# EastEnders
## THE FIRST 10 YEARS

To my wife, Kerry, with love.

# EastEnders

## THE FIRST 10 YEARS

A Celebration
by
Colin Brake

BBC BOOKS

## Acknowledgements

There are many people who need to be thanked for their part in making this book possible, not least of whom are the cast and crew of EastEnders, past, present and future, whose work is the subject of this celebration.

I must thank Leonard Lewis who was Executive Producer of the programme when this project started and whose initial enthusiasm for it made the book a reality, also Barbara Emile who became Series Producer as the book entered production, and whose help and support in the latter stages of this project has been equally important, I would also like to say a special thank you to Keith Harris, the genius who designed Albert Square, whose visual contributions to this book are much appreciated. Thank you, too, to all those who gave their time and allowed me to interview them for this book especially Julia Smith, Tony Holland, Keith Harris, Chris Murison, Vanessa De Souza, Mark Sendell and Paul Carney.

For the record the Producers of EastEnders 1985–1994 were: Julia Smith, Tony Virgo, Mike Gibbon, Michael Ferguson, Corinne Hollingworth, Richard Bramall, Pat Sandys, Leonard Lewis, Helen Greaves, Barbara Emile, Diana Kyle, Mike Hudson and Jane Fallon. The Script and/or Story Editors, Storyline Editors, and Script Consultants of EastEnders 1985–1994 were: Tony Holland, Morag Bain, Estelle Daniel, John Maynard, Bill Lyons, Jane Galletly, Jane Harris, Colin Brake, Anna Price, Alison Davies, Sebastian Secker Walker, Andrew Holden, Barry Thomas, Sallie Aprahamian, Rio Fanning, Lilie Ferrari, Tim Vaughan, Michael Le Moignan, Barbara Emile, Yvon Grace, Harriet Longfield, Jane Fallon, Glen Noble, Tony McHale, Ian Aldwinckle, Nicholas Hicks-Beach, Janet Goddard, Karen Rigby, Heather Peace, John Yorke, Louise Berridge, Helena Pope and Rachel Pole.

In the absence of a formal Bibliography, I would also like to acknowledge a couple of previous books on this subject: EastEnders – The Inside Story by Julia Smith and Tony Holland (BBC Books); The EastEnders Handbook by Hilary Kingsley (BBC Books) and The EastEnders Programme Guide by Josephine Munro (Virgin).

Finally I'd like to thank all those at BBC Books who've made this such a pleasurable experience; the ever-supportive trio in the publicity office at EastEnders (Sara Bache, Hellen Martin and Fenella Mantle; and last, but by no means least Carolyn Weinstein and Lorraine Newman at the EastEnders offices in Elstree whose job descriptions ('Series Producer's Assistant' and 'Research Secretary' respectively) do not even begin to reveal their central importance to the smooth running of the programme.

# Contents

# Introduction

I'm a lucky man. In 1985, when *EastEnders* started, I thought it was the best thing on television. At the time I worked in a library and, although I dreamed of working in television, I had no idea how to make that dream a reality. Eighteen months later I started work on *EastEnders*, as the programme's first historian and archivist. Within six months I had become a trainee script editor on the programme. When *EastEnders* celebrates its tenth birthday in February 1995 I will have been fortunate enough to have enjoyed an association with the programme that spans eight-and-a-half years. In that time I've been a script editor, a story editor and storyline editor for the show, and now I'm one of the team who actually write the programme. That's why I'm a lucky man.

From the days when Julia Smith, as producer, and Tony Holland, as script editor, were in charge, up to now with the programme going out three times every week, I've been in a position to know the inside story of the first decade of *EastEnders*. I think it's a story worth celebrating and that's why I've written this book, to celebrate ten years of *EastEnders* and to give a glimpse *behind* the screen, to see how it all happened.

Here's to the next ten years!

Colin Brake

# The *EastEnders* Story

*EastEnders* is ten years old! It hardly seems possible now, but back at the beginning of 1985, the word 'EastEnders', with the distinctive second capital letter 'E' and no dividing space or hyphen, was unheard of.

No one knew about the existence of a London borough called Walford, or of a Luxford and Copley public house called The Queen Vic. No one knew a Den and Angie Watts, or a Pete and Kathy Beale. No one had ever shopped in Turpin Road Market.

That all changed at 7.00 p.m. on Tuesday 19 February when the haunting sound of Simon May's *EastEnders* theme was broadcast for the first time. The front cover of the *Radio Times* for that week proclaimed: 'The EastEnders are here ...' and, after months of hard work behind the scenes, the BBC's first year-round, bi-weekly serial since the early seventies was finally on the screen.

Invited by a series of posters, on-screen trails and pages of press coverage, seventeen million people tuned in for that first episode. The figures have gone up and down many times since then, sometimes due to seasonal fluctuations, sometimes boosted by particularly gripping or controversial storylines, but whatever the actual figures the programme has been one of the BBC's most consistently popular shows since its launch.

A television programme, however, does not appear on the screens overnight, especially one that is as complicated and demanding to produce as a twice-weekly drama serial. The real beginnings of *EastEnders* can be traced back much further than February 1985. When *was EastEnders* born? Was it December 1984 when recording began, or April 1984 when the first scripts were commissioned? Or was it March 1984 when the characters were created by Julia Smith and Tony Holland in a holiday apartment in Lanzarote, or March 1983, when Julia and Tony were first asked to work on a bi-weekly serial for the BBC?

The real answer to the question is—all of the above. But to understand fully why *EastEnders* came to be, we need to go back a little further still to recall the world of television it was born into. British television in the early eighties was very different to the way it is today. Back then satellite television was still a thing of the future, and cable seemed even further off. The television industry in Britain had been fairly balanced for nearly fifteen years, since the introduction of BBC2 back in 1967, but that all changed in 1982, with the appearance of the fourth channel.

## The arrival of Channel Four, and *Brookside*

Channel Four was designed from the outset to be an alternative television choice, allowing different views and perspectives to reach the television audience. For many it was seen as a high-brow intellectual channel, providing specialist coverage of various issues for numerous minority groups, but

at the same time Jeremy Issacs, the first boss of the new channel, knew that they had to attract large popular audiences as well.

One of its strategies was to build into its schedules a bi-weekly soap—*Brookside*. Created by Phil Redmond, the man who had devised the successful long-running BBC children's drama *Grange Hill*, *Brookside* has been a consistent rating success for the youngest British channel. The reason is simple—audiences like continuous serials, long-running sagas that take a group of characters through a protracted storyline. They enjoy the way characters and situations can grow, change and evolve over a period of time, and take pleasure in the development of a series' own sense of history.

There's nothing new in this, of course; in many ways the magazine serializations of nineteenth-century writers like Charles Dickens and Arthur Conan Doyle were very similar. In broadcast terms, the earliest serials were to be found on the radio but these soon spread to television. The term 'soap opera' comes to us from those early radio shows in America. Aimed predominantly at a female audience, they were most often sponsored by large soap companies thus creating their name.

These days the term 'soap opera' carries negative overtones, and programmes given the label are seen as cheap and tacky melodramas of little artistic merit. As far as *EastEnders* is concerned, the current series producer, Barbara Emile, is the latest in the long line of dedicated *EastEnders* producers to insist that the programme is a drama *series*, not a soap opera.

**Early television serials**

In Britain, like the United States, it didn't take long for soap operas—or on-going serials, if you prefer—to make the transition from radio to television. As early as 1954 the BBC produced *The Grove Family*, named after the Lime Grove studios where the programmes were made. This series featured stories about an average family coping with the trials and tribulations of everyday life a decade after the end of the Second World War. Like many shows that followed it, the programme attracted a great deal of mail, much of it from viewers who seemed convinced that the family in the show really existed. The series was also followed by the popular Press, which liked to fill its pages with gossip about the characters and the star, as still happens with *EastEnders* today.

The grand old lady of the genre in this country is, of course, Granada's *Coronation Street*. Initially given only a thirteen-week run in 1960, starting on 9 December, it reached the rest of the network the following year and has been going strong ever since. During the sixties the BBC tried to emulate the success of their northern rivals, with shows like *Compact*, *United* and *The Newcomers*, but none of these proved to be real long-runners. When *Compact* closed down, the creators took their next idea to ATV and *Crossroads* was born. (Interestingly, one of the directors on *The Newcomers* was Julia Smith, later the co-creator of *EastEnders*, and one of the stars of the programme was a young Wendy Richard.)

Throughout the seventies *Coronation Street* and *Crossroads* reigned supreme, supported by

*Emmerdale Farm* from 1971, although at first this was a serial which only ran for part of the year. By the eighties the BBC were beginning to struggle to keep an equal share of the viewers. The BBC management realized that they needed to find some new popular programmes to bring the viewers back to the BBC.

## Competition from ITV

In 1984 the BBC was greatly embarrassed by the criticism it received when it screened an American mini-series, *The Thorn Birds*. The BBC's critics saw the imported programme as a prime example of the kind of programme the BBC *shouldn't* be screening—it was mocked for being tacky, shallow and melodramatic. Meanwhile ITV were busy screening Granada's *The Jewel in the Crown*, a lavishly produced adaptation of Paul Scott's 'Raj Quartet' books, to great critical acclaim. Many pointed out the irony of an ITV company producing drama of the kind the BBC used to be famous for. No doubt the BBC were further embarrassed by research which showed that audiences believed that the BBC *had* made *The Jewel in the Crown!*

One of the many ideas considered by BBC executives to deal with the problem was the possibility of re-entering the soap market. They only had to look at the weekly ratings of Granada's *Coronation Street* to see the potential merits of such a programme, and the recent evidence of the relative success of *Brookside* on the minority Channel Four must have given further support to

the idea. The BBC had experimented with the form of a bi-weekly serial for a number of years, screening such programmes as *Angels*, *Triangle* and even *Doctor Who* twice-weekly for limited runs in early evening slots. Now they decided to go the whole hog and find a programme to fill such a slot all year round. Controller of BBC1 at the time, Alan Hart, and Head of Series and Serials, David Reid, were the prime movers in the plan. It was they who turned to producer Julia Smith and script editor Tony Holland to provide the creative force to launch the new BBC soap.

The 'Guvnors': co-creators Julia Smith and Tony Holland with some of the many industry awards that *EastEnders* won in its first three years.

## Julia Smith steps in

On 14 March 1983 Julia and Tony, who were working in Cardiff on a series called *The District Nurse*, were called to a meeting with David Reid in London. There they were asked to take on the new soap project.

Julia Smith was then a successful producer, having started as a director on episodes of *Doctor Who*, *Doctor Finlay's Casebook* and *Z-Cars*. It was on *Z-Cars* that she met Tony Holland who, after starting his career as an actor, had turned to script editing and writing. In the seventies, as producer of *Angels*, Julia managed to persuade the BBC to turn the series of fifty-minute episodes into a serial running twice-weekly for sixteen weeks of the year. To help her engineer this major change in format she sought out Tony Holland, knowing that he shared her vision of strong, fast-moving, gritty drama. No doubt it was their shared experience on the twice-weekly *Angels* that best qualified them to take on the new soap.

During the rest of 1983, a series of meetings was held as the mammoth task of working out the logistics of producing a new drama, twice a week for fifty-two weeks of the year, was discussed. Meanwhile the BBC commissioned some pilot scripts. A number of ideas for the series had been thrown up and two of them were selected for this next stage of development. One was set in a shopping arcade, the other in a mobile-home park. Although both ideas had interesting elements, Julia and Tony had doubts about them. The shopping arcade idea was fraught with expensive technical considerations and the mobile-home park

didn't seem to have the longevity needed by a soap. The producer and script editor were equally determined to reject both ideas, but it was off-screen events at the end of 1983 that dictated the project's next turn.

Two events were to influence the next stage in the birth of *EastEnders*. First, the BBC's Director of Resources, Michael Checkland, was investigating the possibility of buying the old ATV studios at Elstree in Hertfordshire. The site offered a number of possibilities for the BBC, not the least of which was having the capacity to become the base for the new bi-weekly serial. The other major move was David Reid's, who left his post as Head of Series and Serials at the end of the year. His replacement was Jonathan Powell, a drama producer, renowned for high-quality productions like *The Mayor of Casterbridge* and *Tinker, Tailor, Soldier, Spy*.

At the first meeting with Jonathan Powell, Julia and Tony were hoping for an opportunity to reject the idea of the mobile-home park and wanted to suggest a London-based soap as an alternative. As luck would have it, Jonathan was thinking along similar lines.

What happened next has the feel of legend rather than fact, but it did actually happen. On Wednesday 1 February 1984 Julia and Tony had gone to collect some market research that had been commissioned by the Drama Department to test the appeal of a soap set in the south of England. Returning to the BBC Drama offices in Shepherds Bush, they dropped into Jonathan Powell's outer office to pass on the results. There they were told that Jonathan needed the format for the soap that night—he had a meeting with

Alan Hart, the Controller of BBC1, the next morning and wanted the format as a selling document. With less than an hour before Jonathan would be leaving the office, Julia and Tony took themselves across the road to a local wine bar and wrote a 300-word format. The next day Alan Hart accepted the new idea. All they needed now was a name. *Round the Square* and *London Pride* were considered but, for the time being, they decided to go with *East 8*, E8 being the London postal district of Hackney.

Just two weeks earlier the BBC had formally taken possession of the old Elstree Studios, in Hertfordshire, and it was decided that the new BBC Elstree Centre would be the home of the new soap.

The rest of 1984 was a blur of creative activity. The year started with the BBC moving into the abandoned ATV studios

**Above and overleaf:**
One time home to *Auf Wiedersehen, Pet* and *The Muppet Show*, the Elstree site became BBC property in January 1984 and the construction of Albert Square, under the watchful eye of series designer Keith Harris, could begin.

and ended with the first recordings of Albert Square. In between, many, many people worked their fingers to the bone to turn the dream into reality. Early in the year Keith Harris joined the team as the production designer. With Julia and Tony he toured the East End, taking endless photos and notes. For a while they looked for actual locations in the East End in which to shoot the exterior Walford scenes, but the cost in time and money of transporting cast and crew to and from the East End on a regular basis would have been prohibitive. Another solution had to be found. In the early spring of 1984 Julia took her two colleagues on a visit to Elstree. Jonathan Powell had suggested that they should have a look at the back lot at Elstree. Sited beyond the main studio buildings, up against the perimeter fence of the site, the lot was a large open space, covered in rubble and sand. It had last been used in the ITV show *Auf Wiedersehen, Pet* as a building site supposedly set in Germany.

Standing on the abandoned site, Julia, Tony and Keith realized that the solution to their problems was right beneath their feet. They would build a permanent set for Albert Square here, on the same site as the studios which would contain the interior sets.

## Getting down to work

The next task was to flesh out that original format and create the characters. With constant phone calls and questions punctuating their working day in London, Tony and Julia decided to get away from it all. They arranged a two-week break in Lanzarote, but not as a vacation—they went there to work. For two weeks they worked flat out, creating, in a flurry of activity, twenty-three character biographies, broad storylines for three years and detailed ones for the first twenty episodes. It was certainly no holiday!

While the framework of Albert Square rose from the ashes of a German building site on the lot at Elstree, Julia and Tony began the next stage of planning. Tony began to round up a team of writers, knowing that the turnover of writers would be fast and furious on a programme like *EastEnders*. Some of the writers were people he or Julia had worked with before on other programmes, some came with recommendations from other similar shows, and a few were writers new to television.

Elsewhere Julia was dealing with her side of operations, starting the process of casting the roles and finding directors. Julia knew that she would need to find actors and

directors of a special breed to survive the *EastEnders* assault course *and* make good programmes. The director chosen for the first pair of *EastEnders* episodes was Matthew Robinson, a young energetic director with a flair for stylish, fast-moving camerawork. Now a successful producer, Matthew makes the popular children's drama *Byker Grove*.

Among the many dates that lay claim to being the birthday of *EastEnders* we can add 4 April 1984, which was the first point at which freelance writers were formally involved with the project. Without writers the programme wouldn't exist; once those first episodes were commissioned the programme was really underway. The first four writers were Jane Hollowood, Valerie Georgeson, Bill Lyons and Gerry Huxham.

## A vital last-minute change

With scripts and a cast in place, production could begin in December 1984 with a read-through of the first six episodes. For the first time, Julia and Tony got a taste of what *EastEnders* would sound like; for the first time, all the characters began to interact. The only niggle was in the casting of the key role of Angie Watts; in the first rehearsals the actress they had cast seemed to be struggling to

find the character. With days to go before the first shooting began, Julia Smith took the difficult decision to recast the role. One of the hardest parts of a producer's job is telling an actor that their contract is not going to be renewed and that the programme will be going on without them; it is even harder when the programme hasn't even started. Although unbearable for the poor actress who lost the role of Angie, the crisis proved to be an important turning point for *EastEnders*. The new Angie, Anita Dobson, seemed to have a real instinct for the character, and when she joined the cast, the first *EastEnders* company was complete.

## *EastEnders* gathers momentum

Like a jumbo jet screaming down a runway, picking up enough speed to take off, *EastEnders* began hurtling through time towards the launch date. The constant cycle of production began to settle down into a hectic but organized routine. And on Tuesday 19 February 1985, the jet left the ground and *EastEnders* finally took off. And for the viewers who took to this new serial, *that* was the day it was born. For them the story was just beginning, a story that is still being told today, ten years later...

# Round the Square

Where is Walford? As with most questions about *EastEnders* there are a number of answers; answers that relate both to the fiction of the *EastEnders* stories and the reality of *EastEnders* the television production. The London Borough of Walford, E20, is a product of both fiction and reality.

### Creating Walford

When Julia Smith, Tony Holland, and Jonathan Powell first started talking about 'the East End' as a possible setting for the new soap, the phrase 'where that bend in the river occurs' was used. This is the Isle of Dogs, containing Millwall and Cubitt Town, but Walford is not to be found there. The real East End of London lies further north: Poplar, Hackney, Limehouse, Mile End, Bethnal Green and Bow, and it was to these places that Julia, Tony and their designer, Keith Harris, went to research the East End.

The Walford that they created between them had elements from all these areas; the multi-cultural populations, the high unemployment, the many social problems, the street markets and the rough but warm Cockney sense of humour. One possible real location for Albert Square was Fassett Square in Hackney but, when the decision was made to build a permanent set at the Elstree Centre, Keith Harris

The buildings on the lot existed as detailed plans before any building began – here Julia Smith checks some plans for expansion with Keith Harris.

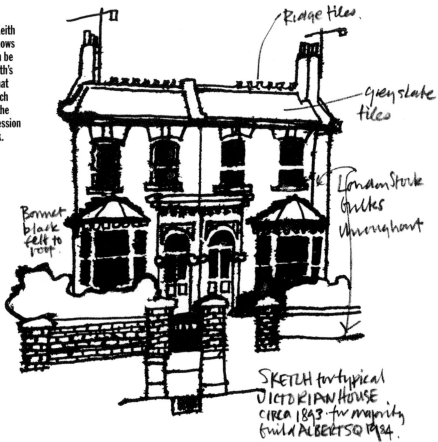

This annotated sketch by Keith Harris, dated June 1984, shows the kind of houses that can be found in Albert Square. Keith's comments show exactly what materials he wanted for each part of the building, while the sketch itself gives an impression of how he wanted it to look.

*Ridge tiles.*

*grey slate tiles*

*London Stock Bricks throughout*

*Bonnet black felt to roof.*

*SKETCH for typical VICTORIAN HOUSE CIRCA 1893. for majority build ALBERT SQ 1934.*

switched his attention to taking reams of precise architectural details from various locations in the East End to incorporate into his designs for Walford.

The reality of Walford is to be found in the numerous studio sets that give the illusion of being the various living rooms, kitchens and hallways of the houses and flats in the Square and the interiors of the other places in Walford such as The Queen Vic bar, the café and the launderette. It is also found on the lot, the vast outdoor set, that contains the exterior shells of the houses and buildings, as well as the roads and rail bridges that give the Square its shape.

The lot is a wonderful piece of design, like a section of a model village built for a giant. The drains on the lot really work, so when rain falls it runs away in a natural manner. Although many walls are no more than painted marine plywood mounted on metal frames, other parts of the Square are made of real bricks and concrete. One of the public telephone boxes in Turpin Road really works. Reality and fiction blend at each step you take on the lot. It is possible to stand in Bridge Street and believe, for a moment, that you really are in the East End rather than on a television set in Hertfordshire.

# Albert Square, Walford E20

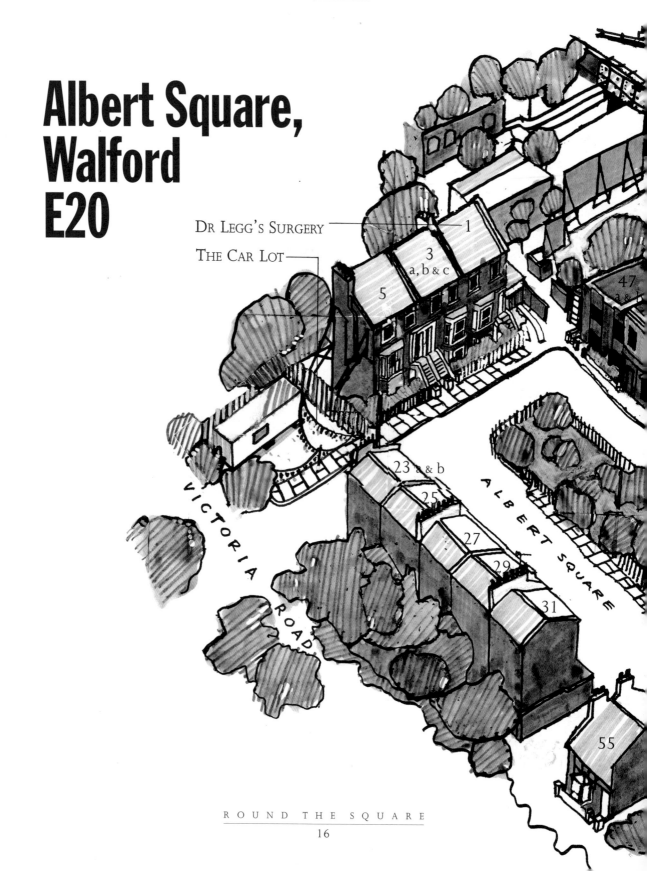

Dr Legg's Surgery
The Car Lot

1
3
a, b & c
5
47
a & b
23 a & b
25
27
29
31
55

VICTORIA ROAD

ALBERT SQUARE

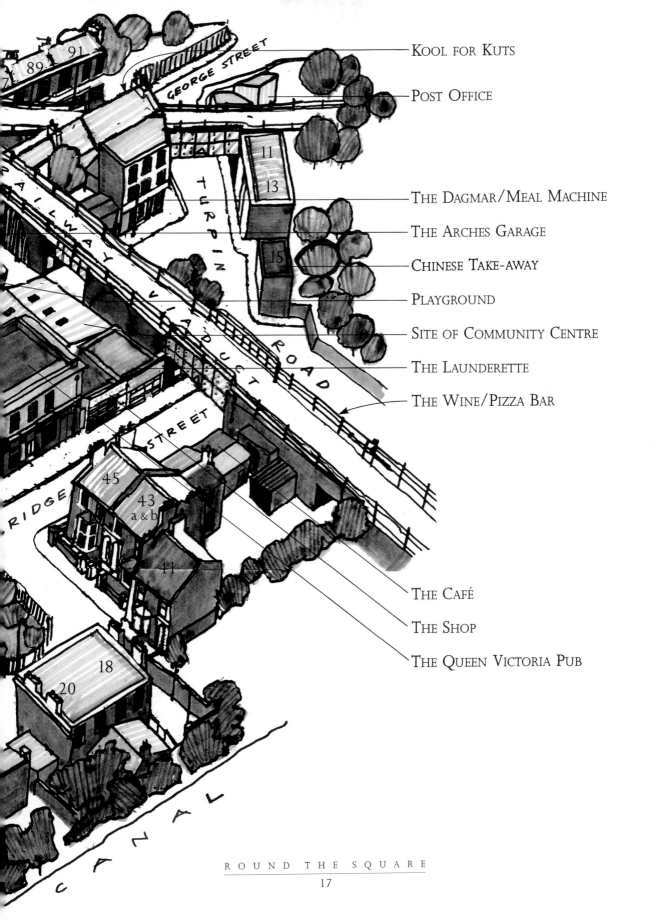

KOOL FOR KUTS

POST OFFICE

THE DAGMAR/MEAL MACHINE

THE ARCHES GARAGE

CHINESE TAKE-AWAY

PLAYGROUND

SITE OF COMMUNITY CENTRE

THE LAUNDERETTE

THE WINE/PIZZA BAR

THE CAFÉ

THE SHOP

THE QUEEN VICTORIA PUB

## Creating Albert Square itself

The history of the Square begins with a sketch, scratched into the sand left on the lot by *Auf Wiedersehen, Pet*. When Julia, Tony and Keith Harris first looked around the lot and thought about the possibility of building a section of the East End right there in Elstree, they grabbed a stick and sketched out the shape of the Square, indicating with broad strokes where roads, houses and buildings would go. Just a few months later, this vision began to turn into reality.

The lot was first unveiled to the Press in October 1984, when the cast assembled in Albert Square for a Press photo-call, although the Square that was invaded by the Press on that day was not exactly complete. For the first year or so of its existence Albert Square was missing a side; only three sides of the Square had been built, along with Bridge Street.

The Square wasn't completed until the summer of 1986, when further building work created the 'fourth wall'. This produced the house that the Butchers now live in (number 41), the Bed and Breakfast plus the house next to it and, in the far corner of the Square, a house which backed

Left: An early view of Bridge Street showing Pete's van parked in its normal spot and the original open-fronted version of the shop.
Below: Albert Square — or more accurately the three sides of the square that were built in 1984 in phase one of the development of the *EastEnders* lot.

on to the Square, facing out on to the largely invisible Victoria Road.

The following year saw the third major expansion of the lot, with the building of the rest of Turpin Road, the development of the wine bar under the arches, the Chinese take-away, the betting shop, and the new Dagmar pub. As a final touch, Keith Harris noticed that the Elstree buildings which housed the *EastEnders* vehicles, including the red Routemaster bus that is often used, could be seen at the end of Turpin Road. Keith stuck up a London Transport sign saying 'Walford Garage' to make the existing Elstree building part of the fictional world.

For a while the only changes on the lot were small: number 43 was converted into two flats, a Portakabin was introduced on the site in the corner of the Square that had originally been a used tyre yard and, some time later, a garage was created under the arches opposite the Community Centre for the new characters Phil and Grant Mitchell.

The last major expansion to date has been the George Street development, built at the end of Turpin Road, which extends the range of shops and housing available for characters to live and work in. This was done in anticipation of an influx of new characters when the programme began to be shown three times a week. The expansion was first discussed at the end of 1992 but building didn't begin until August 1993. With this expansion the lot is virtually full up—for now, this is as big as it will get. Other parts of Walford will continue to be seen, however, as they have in the past by using real locations. Many parts of Borehamwood, Edgware, Elstree and Radlett have doubled for bits of Walford before, and no doubt they will again in the future.

**A Keith Harris sketch showing the fourth side of the Square which was added in 1986, phase two of the lot's development.**

# The Guided Tour

### 55 Victoria Road

Originally the home of the Karims, this was later bought by Rachel Kominski. Since she left the Square the house has been rented by Michelle Fowler, who has lived here with her daughter Vicki, first sharing with Shelley, and then with her brother Mark.

### 23 Albert Square

This is a council property, consisting of two flats. After the death of Reg Cox, single mum Mary Smith and her baby Annie moved in. The downstairs flat was the original home of Sue and Ali Osman and their baby Hassan. When they moved out, Dot Cotton moved in, having previously lived in the same tower block as Pete Beale. Later, Dot did a swap with her neighbour, Tom Clements. Mo Butcher lived in the upper flat for a while, and took in Trevor Short as a lodger. Disa O'Brian and her baby stayed in the flat briefly, then newly-weds Ricky and Sam Butcher squatted in the flat. Since their eviction by the council the house has been empty, presumably awaiting council renovation and repair.

### 25 Albert Square

Originally Tom Clements' house, this was then Dot's home until she left the Square in 1993. During that time she had numerous guests, including her errant husband Charlie, her evil son Nick, her friend Ethel and her lodger Donna, who died in the house. Since Dot left a new family, the Jacksons, have moved in and, like Dot, they too previously lived on 'the estate'.

### 27 Albert Square

Also a council house, this was home to the Tavernier family from 1990 until 1994, when Jules, the only member of the family remaining in Walford, decided to ask for something smaller.

### 20 Albert Square

The Bed and Breakfast, run by the never-seen Doris for many years, this house was taken over by Frank and Pat Butcher when they gave up the Vic. They also owned the house next door, number 18, which they actually lived in.

### 41 Albert Square

Although added to the Square in the first expansion in 1986, it wasn't until 1993 that anyone was featured living here. This is the new home of the Butcher family. Along with Michelle Fowler, Pat is probably the character who has lived in the greatest number of Albert Square locations.

### 43 Albert Square

Originally known as 'the little blue house' to the writers, this is one of the most lived-in places in Albert Square. First owned by Andy O'Brien and Debbie Wilkins, Debbie sold the house to James Willmott-Brown after Andy's death. When James moved to live 'over the shop' at the Dagmar, he had the house converted into flats. The downstairs flat, 43a, was bought by Den Watts for Sharon, Michelle and Vicki to live in. The top flat was bought by Joanne, the mysterious manager of the wine bar. She sold it to Julie Cooper, who eventually sold it

to Phil Mitchell. Meanwhile, Grant Mitchell bought the downstairs flat from Sharon in 1990. This was then sold to Frank and Pat, who lived here until October 1993, when they sold it to Phil, who meanwhile had sold the upstairs flat to Gita and Sanjay Kapoor. In 1994 Kathy Beale moved into the lower flat with Phil.

## 45 Albert Square

A council house, originally rented in Lou Beale's name, this has been the Beale family home for decades, all the way back to the Second World War, as we saw in the 1988 Christmas special 'Civvy Street'. Mark and Michelle grew up here, and now the house is home to Arthur, Pauline, Auntie Nellie and Martin. Guests here include Naima Jeffery, Pete, Aidan and Mandy.

## The Queen Victoria public house

A Luxford and Copley pub for many years, Den and Angie Watts were the first tenants we knew. It was never explicitly stated in the programme but it was suggested that Den's father may have been the publican here years before. After Angie and Den split he ran it on his own for a while. The next tenants were Frank and Pat Butcher, followed by the unlucky Eddie Royle. With the help of Grant and Phil, Sharon bought the freehold of the pub in 1990, and it has remained a free house since then. Grant and Sharon are now buying back Phil's share.

## 47 and 47a Albert Square

The ground-floor flat was owned and lived in by Alan McIntyre, a local builder. He also owned the upstairs flat, which he rented to Sue and Ali. Later Mark and Steve rented this flat and, after Steve left, Nigel moved in. Whether McIntyre still owns the properties is unknown.

Incidentally, one of the quirks of Albert Square is the numbering of the houses—given the size of the Square, house numbers should never have got as high as 47!

## 1 Albert Square

This is Dr Legg's house. Originally he lived in Islington and only held his surgery here. In those days he rented the two flats above the surgery to Ethel and Lofty. When Lofty married Michelle they both lived here for a while. When Ethel moved into sheltered housing, Dr Legg decided to move in and lived here with his nephew, David, who joined him in the practice for a time. Dr Legg now lives here alone.

## 3 Albert Square

This was Tony Carpenter's house, which he was converting into flats when the series began. He and Kelvin lived here when the building work was finished. When Tony decided to return to the Caribbean, he left Kelvin in the basement flat and sold the top flat to Colin Russell. Colin later rented the flat to Rod and Hazel, then Ian and Cindy, who live here today. The middle flat was rented by Carmel, who lived here with her husband Matthew. The basement flat was rented by Kathy for a

The *EastEnders* cast, around the piano in The Queen Vic pub, circa late 1985. Already a few new faces have joined the originals including Dot Cotton (June Brown) and Simon 'Wicksy' Wicks (Nick Berry).

number of years. The current occupants of the basement flat and the middle flat are unknown.

## 5 Albert Square

The house, propped up by raking shores after wartime bomb damage, has been derelict throughout the programme's history, and has been used as a squat by a number of characters including Donna, Rod, Mandy and Aidan. In 1993 the house was bought by Richard Cole, and the following year he converted it into bedsits.

## 7 Albert Square

When the programme started this was a derelict tyre yard but when Chris Smith, Mary's father, decided to set up business he acquired the site and installed a Portakabin to serve as his office. When Chris's haulage firm failed, Frank Butcher took on the site to sell second-hand cars.

## The shop, 71 Bridge Street

Originally an open-fronted grocery store, Naima and Saeed Jeffery had recently inherited it when the programme began. When their marriage failed Naima reshaped it as a late-night convenience store and named it 'First Till Last'. After Naima left to get married, the Karim family took it over. After them, unseen relatives of the family took over the shop but by 1993 it had been added to the interests of Mr Papadopolous, who also owns the launderette. He employed Mrs Andreos to manage the shop.

## The launderette, 73 Bridge Street

This was owned by Mr Papadopolous (or Opodopolus, according to Dot), who died in 1992 and left the business to his son. Over the years the launderette has given

employment to Dot, Ethel, Mary, Arthur, Pauline, Michelle, Nigel and Carol.

## The café, Bridge Street

This was Al's café, run by Sue and Ali Osman. It was also the home of OzCabs, the taxi firm run by Ali and his brother Mehmet. Ali finally sold the café to Ian Beale, who ran it for a while to make money to invest in his catering business. Ian sold it to Frank, Pauline and Kathy. Kathy later bought Pauline out, and in 1994 Phil purchased Frank's share.

## The market, Bridge Street and Turpin Road

Turpin Road Market is a long-established street market, licensed and run by Walford Council. Originally it only just spread into Bridge Street by a few feet, under the bridge,

but over the years it has spread further along Bridge Street towards the Square. The Beale fruit and veg stall, which has been in the family for over three generations, was never officially part of the market, although the licence to trade is issued by the council. When the series opened the stall was still officially owned by Lou, although Pete and Kathy had run it since their marriage. After Lou's death it was left jointly to the twins, Pete and Pauline, with Arthur joining Pete on the stall for a while, as Pauline's representative. Pete then bought out his sister and was sole owner when he died, so the stall was left jointly to Ian, his son by Kathy, and David Wicks, his son by his first wife Pat. Ian and David sold it to Mark Fowler, which would probably have been fine with Pete, as it was Mark who he asked to look after the stall before he went on the run.

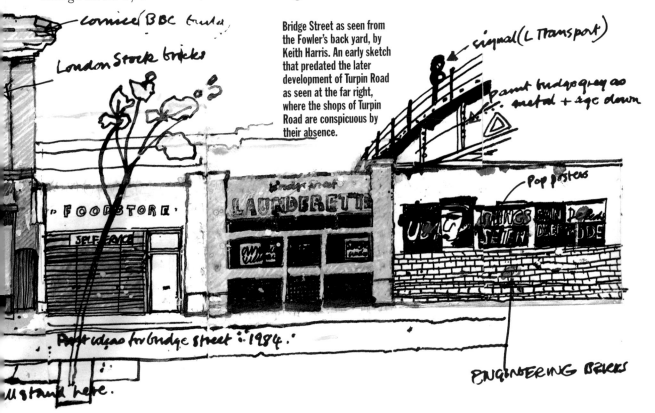

Bridge Street as seen from the Fowler's back yard, by Keith Harris. An early sketch that predated the later development of Turpin Road as seen at the far right, where the shops of Turpin Road are conspicuous by their absence.

In Turpin Road itself we must assume that the market extends further up the road past the wine bar. This section of Turpin Road has never been built or seen, as that area of the lot is given over to Arthur's allotment, which exists some way from Albert Square in the fictional world.

### The wine bar, Turpin Road

The wine bar in Turpin Road was first referred to in 1986, as Henry's, a rival to the Vic. When Den left the Vic he was set up by the Firm as the manager of the wine bar, now renamed Strokes. After the demise of this enterprise, the building became a pizza restaurant, where Steve Elliot found work. Incidentally, the building is housed in one of the arches of the railway viaduct, so it must be an odd choice for a quiet night out! The basement of the wine bar was used by the Firm for illegal gambling and in 1994 by Ian Beale as the offices for his new loan business.

### Chinese take-away, 15 Turpin Road

The Green Dragon has never really been featured, although when characters talk about getting a take-away Chinese meal this is probably where they go.

### Betting shop, 13 Turpin Road

Like the Chinese take-away next door, there is no interior for this location built on the

A Keith Harris sketch of the Turpin Road development showing the new pub, The Dagmar.

lot. However, the interior has been seen as a studio set on occasion.

## Video Shop, 11 Turpin Road

This is designed more like the shop in Bridge Street, and the interior can be used on the lot. Originally a video shop, it was then used as the site of Julie's hairdressing salon. When that closed the building was empty for some time before reopening as a video shop. In 1994 Nigel Bates got the job as manager of the shop.

## The Dagmar

Opposite the betting shop is a large building that used to be the Dagmar, *EastEnders'* other pub. James Willmott-Brown got the tenancy of the Dagmar when he left his job as area manager for Luxford and Copley. The studio set for the Dagmar only featured the smaller bar at the Dagmar—an intimate area, decorated in bright green. The other bar, presumably much bigger, was never seen. After Willmott-Brown raped Kathy in the flat above the pub, Den had the place burnt down. A couple of years later, the site was perfect for Ian Beale's new catering business, the Meal Machine. Since this went belly-up in 1993 the building has remained empty.

## Community Centre/Playground

Between the corner of the Square where Dr Legg's surgery is and Turpin Road there is an alley. On one side of this is the small children's playground, on the other the local Community Centre. This has been seen used for jumble sales, mother and toddler groups and private parties, but the Centre was burnt down in 1992. So far the council has been unable to find the money to rebuild it, but one is planned and will appear in time.

## Garage

At the end of the alley, where the entrance to the Community Centre used to be, there is another arch of the railway viaduct. Through here you reach Turpin Road and find two more phone boxes. Before you go through, however, you can also see the Mitchell brothers' garage, which is in the arch to the left of the bridge.

## George Street

At the far end of Turpin Road you come to George Street, which runs back almost parallel to Dr Legg's side of the Square, where it must intersect with Victoria Road. On the far side of this street are three houses, which are the remains of a Victorian terrace. All of these have been turned into flats. In the last house, number 87, we know one inhabitant, Natalie. Jules Tavernier moved next door to the ground floor flat at number 89 during 1994. Both flats are council owned. The ground floor flat in the next house was rented by Nigel and Debbie during 1994.

Opposite these houses are two shops. Number 100 used to be a pet shop, but when first seen in early 1994 it had closed down. This became Steve and Della's hairdresser's in the spring of 1994. Next door at number 98 is a second-hand furniture shop. Beyond the junction with Turpin Road is the tiny local Post Office, at number 102 George Street.

# 1985:

# That Was the Year That . . .

The birth of *EastEnders* coincided with a death—the murder of old Reg Cox. Tony Holland and Julia Smith were determined to kick off with a bang, throwing the audience into the middle of life in Walford, and letting them learn about the characters as a number of storylines unfolded. The Reg Cox storyline was a good starting point, allowing various members of the community to be involved with or comment on the rather sad circumstances of the old loner's demise.

After a few weeks of the police investigation, prime suspect Nick Cotton left the Square and in April it was reported that he had been arrested. In July, Dot told us that he had managed to get off on probation, and later in the year he returned to Albert Square. The mystery of Reg Cox's murder was not finally solved until four years later when Nick Cotton confessed to Den in prison that he *had* been responsible.

## Introducing the Fowlers

*EastEnders* was not just about death, it also began with a new life in the Square—the baby being carried by Pauline Fowler. At the age of forty-one, she was rather surprised to be a parent again but her mother had an even stronger reaction; with Arthur jobless, Lou was sure that Pauline couldn't afford another child and told her to 'get rid of it'.

The Fowlers had to work very hard to win Lou round, going as far as arranging a holiday for her in Clacton, with Michelle, in an effort to cheer her up. Eventually Lou relented but, despite the birth of young Martin on 31 July, 1985 was a far from happy year for the family.

Right from the beginning, Mark Fowler was in trouble. A mate of Nick Cotton, he found himself implicated in the murder of Reg Cox. Mark was also tempted into joining the racist organization The New Movement. Fearing the police and Nick Cotton, who was also trying to get him into heroin, Mark ran away from home early in April.

This had not been the original plan for the character but, as soon as the regular gruelling schedule of *EastEnders'* production established itself, it became clear that David Scarboro, the young actor chosen to play Mark Fowler, was not happy in the role. The stress of the very heavy workload, and the sudden fame that came to all the actors in the series, were difficult for the young man to cope with and Julia and Tony decided to write the character out to allow the actor to come to terms with the situation better. This meant a hectic period of rewriting early in 1985 as the first fifty-odd scripts were reworked to accommodate this major change. Many of the stories intended for Mark's character were actually given to Michelle—which partially explains, perhaps, the way that her character became so prominent in that first year.

The two families who were created to form the heart of the programme from its very beginning. Here are the Beales and the Fowlers as they were when viewers first met them in February 1985.

9 8 5 :  T H A T  W A S  T H E  Y E A R  T H A T . . .

29

Kelvin and Ian were other beneficiaries of the rewrites, and later the character of Wicksy was added, earlier than planned, to represent the slightly older male teen that Mark had been intended to portray. Although David Scarboro returned to the programme for a number of short visits over the following three years he was never to return full-time. Sadly, in 1988 he committed suicide. In 1990 the part was recast and Todd Carty joined the programme, developing the rather more mature Mark Fowler that we know today.

Lou continued to be a problem for the Beales and Fowlers and for a while during 1985 she even went to live with Pete and Kathy in the tower block. It only took Michelle moving into her old room, however, to make Lou hurry back to her own house.

One of the reasons that Michelle moved into a room of her own was that she had become pregnant. Early in the year Michelle and her best mate, Sharon, had competed to be Kelvin's girlfriend. Michelle had won—but it didn't last. When she came back from her holiday with her gran, Michelle was full of a holiday romance with a boy called Carlo. At a party, when Michelle was forced to produce this fantasy boyfriend, her cousin Ian roped in a mate to play the role. Unfortunately, Ian's pal had the nickname Spotty, for reasons that became obvious when he was seen.

After the birth of her baby brother, Michelle became fascinated with the company of older men—perhaps she had been put off teenagers after the Spotty incident. She was seen hanging around having late night chats with Tony Carpenter, Ali Osman and Den Watts. In September she realized that she was pregnant. Despite enquiries from all the family, Michelle refused point blank to tell anyone who the father was—not unreasonable when she knew that the only man she had ever had sex with was her best friend's father. When the secret was finally revealed to the audience in October, it became a secret they would share exclusively with Michelle for over a year.

The Fowlers ended the year by finding Mark living in Southend, working as a mechanic on go-carts on the promenade. To their surprise he was living with a Swedish woman, Ingrid, and her two small children who knew Mark as Daddy!

## Life with the Watts

Over at the Vic, Den and Angie started the year celebrating their seventeenth wedding anniversary, but it soon became clear that the marriage was a sham—behind the scenes of the great business partnership there was not much of a relationship going on. Den even managed to wangle a holiday in Spain with his mistress, Jan, on the pretext of checking out a possible time-share holiday home purchase. Angie gave as good as she got and set about seducing Tony Carpenter. With parents like these, it was no surprise that Sharon was a fairly troubled teenager. Set apart from the other kids because Den and Angie sent her to a private school rather than the local comprehensive, she was a bit of a loner. Spoilt rotten by both her parents, Den's 'little princess' was really a little

madam. She toyed with the
idea of going on the Pill
and later flirted outrageously
with Lofty. In December, an
outbreak of petty thieving at
the Vic almost cost Lofty
his job before the real
culprit was revealed
to be Sharon.

In the middle of
the year, aware
that her drink-
ing had be-
come a
problem,
Angie tried
to give it up
but by August
she was drinking
again. As Christmas
approached, Angie
became the first in a
long line of *EastEnders*
characters to come a
cropper by drinking
and driving. Angie
borrowed Den's car
to go to a darts
match and crashed
it on the way home.

**The surprise hit characters of
the show — Angie and Den Watts,
the live-wire couple whose
on/off, love/hate relationship
made The Queen Victoria public
house such an exciting and
unpredictable place to be.**

## Mary Smith arrives

Young homeless mother, Mary Smith, arrived in the Square in March and was befriended by Nick Cotton, who tried to persuade her to go on the game. In May, her father turned up in Walford looking for her and it became clear that she had run away from her parents in Stockport. Mary later became friendly with both Lofty and Pauline, and confessed to the latter that she couldn't read or write. Despite these new friends Mary kept finding herself in bad company—a chance meeting with a stripper, Sheena Mennell, led her to try stripping as a way to earn money. To her horror, at one performance she recognized a man in the audience—Saeed Jeffery who ran the shop, and who was having marital problems with his wife, Naima.

## The Jefferys

Naima and Saeed's marriage was always suspect; we learned that it had been an arranged match, and with both parties being very shy, it was taking them a long time to get to know each other. Naima confessed to her friend Pauline that she and Saeed were not actually sleeping together. The marriage gradually dissolved and, at the end of the year, when Saeed was revealed to be making obscene phone calls to women, he left in disgrace, leaving the business to Naima.

## Ups and downs with the Osmans

At Al's café, over the road from the shop, life was never quiet. It was clear from the beginning of the programme that Sue and Ali had a loud and robust relationship.

Sue and Ali Osman, who could match Den and Angie when it came to marital arguments!

Always a gambler at heart, Ali attempted a money-making chain letter, the Golden Circle, but it never fulfilled its promise. In June we saw Ali go as far as betting his business in a poker game. Amazingly he won, but his euphoria was short-lived as the very next day his baby son Hassan suffered a cot death. A difficult subject, this tragedy was handled very carefully by the production team and research was done about the whole issue of cot deaths. The British Cot Death Foundation feared that a soap opera would trivialize the subject and frighten new parents, but in the end they were very pleased with the way the subject was handled, and provided back-up support after transmission to many viewers who wanted more information on the subject.

## The Carpenters

Tony Carpenter was separated from his wife, Hannah, and moved into Albert Square to renovate the house he had bought, number 3. His son, Kelvin, moved in with him, and became a close friend of Ian, Sharon and Michelle. Tony had a brief fling with Angie, and he was very hurt when she ended it. Later in the year there were signs of a possible reconciliation between Hannah and Tony, but Kelvin was disappointed when it was revealed that Hannah had a new man in her life, a lawyer called Neville.

## The Beales

Pete Beale started the year as happy as a sandboy but it couldn't last. A good mate of Den's, he provided his pal with the odd alibi to Angie whenever Den needed to slip off to see Jan. He was also worried about his son's interest in cooking—Pete felt that it wasn't the right kind of interest for a man. To please his dad, Ian took up boxing and even won a fight at a local club. After the fight, however, Ian was set upon by his opponent's mates and decided to hang up his gloves.

Pete was further troubled when Nick Cotton broke into Dr Legg's surgery looking for drugs and stole a look at some confidential medical records. He used the information he had unearthed to try to blackmail Kathy Beale. Kathy was finally forced to tell her husband the secret she had kept for years—that she had been raped when she was fourteen and the

Odd job man, Tony Carpenter and his teenage son Kelvin arrived in Albert Square to make over number 3 and start a new life . . .

The shop in Bridge Street was run by Saeed and Naima Jeffery but their arranged marriage was never strong.

## Comings 'n' Goings 1985

In the first few weeks of *EastEnders* we were gradually introduced to the regular characters. These may be considered the originals and were Pauline (Wendy Richard), Arthur (Bill Treacher), Michelle (Susan Tully) and Mark Fowler (David Scarboro); Pete (Peter Dean), Kathy (Gillian Taylforth), Lou (Anna Wing) and Ian Beale (Adam Woodyatt); Den (Leslie Grantham), Angie (Anita Dobson) and Sharon Watts (Letitia Dean); Ali (Nejdet Salih) and Sue (Sandy Ratcliff) Osman; Tony (Oscar James) and Kelvin Carpenter (Paul Medford); Naima (Shreela Ghosh) and Saeed Jeffery (Andrew Johnson); Andy O'Brien (Ross Davidson) and Debbie Wilkins (Shirley Cheriton); Mary (Linda Davidson) and Annie Smith (Samantha Crown); Ethel Skinner (Gretchen Franklin); Dr Harold Legg (Leonard Fenton); and, finally, Nick Cotton (John Altman).

As a key part of making Walford feel real, Julia Smith wanted to feature certain supporting artists on a regular basis to give credibility to the fictional Albert Square. Many of these background performers have remained with the show for all of its ten years. Amongst those seen in the first year were Big Ron (Ron Tarr) on the pots and pans stall, Lil (Jeannie Taylore) on the clothes stall, Maude (Doreen Taylor) on the books stall, the milkman (Michael Leader) and the postman (Ali Baba).

The first departure, of course, was poor old Reg Cox. At the conclusion of the second episode we learned that he had died in hospital, turning Det. Sgt Rich's investigation into a murder hunt. It's not surprising,

resulting child had been given up for adoption. This revelation was hard for Pete to take—he couldn't believe that Kathy had never told him this before, and the seeds of their eventual marriage break-up were sown.

Pete's year ended with Christmas at his mum's—and a Boxing Day hangover that would be remembered for a long time. All day Pete was teased about a disgusting party trick which he had performed—writer Tony McHale remembered this running gag and included a reference to it in another script seven years later!

therefore, that next to leave Walford were Nick Cotton, a prime suspect for the murder, and Mark Fowler, who had also been implicated during the police inquiry.

The year saw a couple of visits from people who would later return for longer stays; first, Mary's father Chris (Allan O'Keefe), then later in the year Ali's brother Mehmet (Haluk Bilginer), his wife Guizin (Ishia Bennison) and Mary's stripper friend Sheena Mennell (Dulice Liecier).

There were also a number of additions to the original cast which extended certain families. It wasn't long before we were introduced to Tony Carpenter's estranged wife Hannah (Sally Sagoe) and his daughter Cassie (Delanie Forbes), who managed to age rapidly before her first appearance. In an early episode Kelvin refers to his young sister as being only seven years old, but when the character was actually seen later in the year it was decided to increase the age of the girl to eleven, so a young actress who would be capable of handling the part could be cast.

The most surprising newcomer during 1985 was Dot Cotton—surprising because most people think that she was there from the very beginning. The character had been referred to from the very earliest episodes but we didn't know what she looked like until June Brown first appeared in Episode 40 in July 1985.

The second major arrival during *EastEnders'* first year was Simon 'Wicksy' Wicks, who drove into Albert Square in a bright yellow sports car in Episode 67. If Wicksy had known then the heartache and confusion

New arrival Simon Wicks, better known as 'Wicksy', turned up in October 1985 much to the joy of Pete, who (at the time) thought he was Simon's father.

that would follow him in the ensuing years perhaps he would have driven straight out again, but he didn't, and Walford gained a new pin-up. Nick Berry's portrayal of Wicksy rapidly became a fan-favourite and, unlike some ex-*EastEnders*, Nick took his many followers to his next television role in Yorkshire Television's *Heartbeat*, when he finally left at the end of 1990.

EastEnders
THE FIRST 10 YEARS

## Memorable Episodes 1985

### Episode 1 (19/2/85)
Written by Gerry Huxham, directed by Matthew Robinson, it began with a bang, as a door was forced open and Arthur, Ali and Den stumbled into Reg Cox's flat, where they found the old man lying near-dead in his armchair. Twenty-nine, hectic, loud, lively minutes later the episode ended with an angry Nick Cotton, freshly evicted from the Vic, putting his fist through the glass in one of the pub doors. EastEnders had arrived!

> Reg Cox makes an early exit from *EastEnders* watched by Den, Arthur and Dr Legg in the first ever episode.

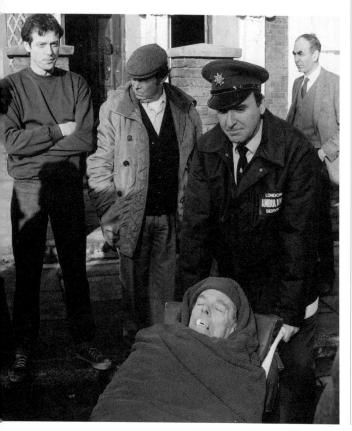

### Episode 36 (20/6/85)
This episode was dominated by the aftershock of the tragic loss of Ali and Sue's small baby, who suffered a cot death. The sudden tragedy came as a surprise to the audience, especially since the bereaved parents were a couple whose feuding, fighting ways had made them appear rather comic in the early episodes of the show. The episode was written by Jane Hollowood.

### Episode 57 (3/9/85)
Here we saw the sad sight of Angie trying to make Den jealous by seducing Lofty, of all people. The episode, which was written by Rosemary Mason, ended with Angie humiliatingly rejected and the jukebox ironically playing 'Stand by your Man'.

### Episode 91 (31/12/85)
Written by Bill Lyons, this featured the first extended use of location work in *EastEnders*, with the crew and cast travelling to Southend to shoot two episodes in which the Fowlers were reunited with Mark. It was quite a shock to see familiar Walford faces in a seaside setting—even if it was the middle of winter!

## Pick of the Year 1985

### Episode 66 (3/10/85)
Written by series co-creator/script editor Tony Holland and directed by co-creator/producer Julia Smith, this was a landmark episode in more ways than one. For a number of weeks the audience had watched as Michelle struggled to cope with

being a pregnant schoolgirl; first refusing to tell anyone, then confessing to her gran (Lou Beale), and throughout it all refusing to tell anyone who the father of the child would be.

Michelle arranged to meet the father in secret. In true whodunnit fashion, three possible suspects were seen leaving the Square in the early half of Episode 66: Tony Carpenter, Ali Osman and Den Watts. Meanwhile Michelle made her way to the rendezvous point, the towpath at the local canal. (In fact, it was the Grand Union Canal at a spot near Alperton in West London.)

As Michelle waited by the canal, a dark car pulled up in a nearby car park. Finally the fluffy white legs of Roly the poodle, bounding out of the car, gave it all away: Den Watts was the man meeting Michelle.

What happened next was also remarkable; the rest of the episode consisted of just one scene. Despite Den's offer to pay for a private operation Michelle refused to have an abortion and told Den that she would go ahead and have the baby. For the first time we saw a vulnerable side to Den; unable to have a child with Angie (Sharon was adopted), it became clear what this baby would mean to the apparently hard-nosed unemotional man.

*The canal bank scene in Episode 66 — one scene, 16 minutes in length, and just the two characters: Michelle and Den.*

For a series that in its first eight months of existence had established a reputation for being fast-moving, rapidly-cut, even breathless in the way it moved from storyline to storyline, scene to scene, this was a bold experiment. It relied on just the one story and two actors to hold the audience for over half an episode.

Leslie Grantham and Susan Tully rose to the occasion, and Tony Holland's sensitive handling of the awkward scene between the teenage girl and the father of her best friend made for one of the highlights of *EastEnders'* first year. The finishing touch was the use of the alternative end title music, a variation of the normal one which replaced the dramatic drum beats with a longer, gentler, semi-romantic piano solo introduction.

EastEnders
**THE FIRST 10 YEARS**

# 1986:

# That Was the Year That . . .

When *EastEnders* began, the Vic was one of a number of meeting places for the characters and the Watts were just one of the families on the Square. Yet somehow during the first year of the show the emphasis shifted to the Vic and to Den and Angie, and the series was dominated by their storylines during 1986.

## Trouble for Den and Angie

The year began quietly with Angie being fined for her driving offence, but things quickly got moving when Angie booked a drag act to play at the Vic. The drag artiste, John Fisher (David Dale), picked on Pete during his performance and a fight ensued. As Den pulled his friend off the poor performer, his mistress, Jan, appeared in the pub. The physical arrival in the Square of Den's mistress sent his marriage into a new decline; all the while Jan was just an idea, Angie could cope with her, but having her set foot in Walford was something else. Depressed, Angie took a near-lethal cocktail of booze and pills at the end of February. By chance, Den had an argument with Jan and returned to the pub in time to find Angie. She had her stomach pumped and duly recovered, but she was severely shaken when she learnt later that she had only been discovered by accident.

Meanwhile in the Square local villains were demanding protection money from the shop and the café. Although some attempt was made, chiefly by Tony Carpenter, to help Naima and the Osmans fight back, the visits continued. In May there was a major bank robbery and some old friends asked Den to look after 'a visitor'. The visitor turned out to be one of the bank-job gang and Den spent an anxious week with the man holed up in the private area of the pub until members of the local Firm smuggled him out. As part-payment for his help, the protection visits ceased.

When she had recovered from her suicide attempt, Angie decided to play Den at his own game and began an affair with Andy O'Brien. Andy and Deb had split up as a couple at this stage but continued to live together in number 43. The affair only lasted about a month; when Andy saw a chance to get back together with Deb he gave Angie the boot.

As the year moved on, Den decided that he had to leave Angie, give up the Vic and marry Jan. He finally got round to telling Angie of his intentions in October. Angie countered this with a bombshell of her own—that she had only six months to live—and Den revised his plans and promised to stay with her. He set about arranging a second honeymoon in Venice. There, by pure coincidence, Den ran into Jan again and sadly Angie saw them together. On the way home from Venice on the Orient Express, the dried-out Angie fell off the

A new Queen at the Vic? Things didn't work out when Den tried to install his mistress Jan in Angie's place behind the bar.

wagon. Drunk, she told the barman all about her Big Lie—she wasn't really dying at all. Further down the

A second honeymoon for Den and Angie in Venice; well, it seemed like a good idea at the time but in practice it hastened the inevitable divorce.

carriage Den heard every word. From that moment on, Den reverted to his original plan and on Christmas Day, with cruel timing, Den gave Angie official notice that he was seeking a divorce. In response, Angie and Sharon walked out of the pub, choosing to take the route through the public areas to cause the most embarrassment possible to Den.

## The Fowlers and the Beales

This was a big year for the Fowlers and the Beales, with Michelle once again at the centre of events. Her pregnancy continued throughout the early months of 1986, and as the day of the birth approached Michelle became increasingly worried about it. In February, Lofty proposed to her but although she turned him down at first eventually she agreed to marry him. Lofty then threw himself into the role of husband-to-be and would-be father. He even tried to get a proper job and applied to be a traffic warden. Unfortunately he failed the medical.

Michelle gave birth to Vicki at the end of May and immediately had to return to her school life as she had to take exams, as did Ian and Sharon. By the end of the month, plans for the wedding were being made, Wicksy was asked to be the best man and Sharon was invited to be the bridesmaid.

The actual wedding, at the end of September, never happened as Michelle decided at the eleventh hour that she couldn't go through with it, and left Lofty waiting at the church. He reacted badly and suffered a severe asthma attack. The week before the wedding, Arthur had announced to a packed Vic that Michelle would be getting a proper reception, but later that night he confessed to Pauline that he had withdrawn the money from the Christmas Club savings scheme that he had been running to pay for it. With Christmas approaching, Arthur realized that he would have to do something to

The decline and fall of Arthur Fowler, he reached rock bottom at Christmas 1986.

explain the lack of money in the account. At the beginning of November Arthur announced that he was going to withdraw the money, then he staged a robbery and claimed that it had been stolen. Being Arthur, he made a poor job of it and, when questioned by the police, he soon confessed. The only bright spot in the Fowlers' lives came in the middle of November when Michelle and Lofty finally did get married at the local register office.

For Arthur, however, the strain was beginning to show. After his arrest he began a slow decline, withdrawing into himself and acting out of character with people. He finally broke down completely on Christmas Day and smashed up the living room.

Ian Beale began to go out with Sharon in the spring, but despite his high score on her 'How to form meaningful relationships' test, the relationship didn't last long. Sharon was a very confused teenager in 1986, seeking guidance from sources as diverse as John Fisher, the drag artiste, and Dot. For a while Sharon took a serious interest in religion. At one point in May, disgusted by the behaviour of her parents, Sharon went missing and hid at Mary's flat.

Lou came into her own when Pat Wicks

appeared in the Square. An old enemy of Pat's mum, Lou was quick to step in when Pat claimed that Pete *wasn't* Wicksy's father. She told Pete to ignore Pat but later in the year, when Pat came back to the Square to stay, we learned that Lou *also* believed Pat to be telling the truth. Lou believed that Pete's elder brother Kenny had fathered Simon, which was why she had banished Kenny from Walford. Pauline overheard the show-down between Pat and Lou and told her twin brother.

the landlady took revenge by sacking Debs. Debbie then began working with her lodger at the shop, which Naima transformed into a late-opening convenience store in July. Andy had an unwanted admirer in Mary, who dropped her punk image to impress him. When he explained that he was only interested in being a friend, Mary's make-up and hair returned to the punk look. Mary then involved herself with Ali's brother Mehmet and, later, Pat, who introduced her to the financial possibilities of 'entertaining' men.

Left: Pete Beale was less than happy to be reacquainted with his first wife Pat Wicks, who returned to Walford with the news that he wasn't Simon's father.

Right: The Walford Carnival gave the regulars a chance to dress up: Arthur came as Roman Walford, Ethel as Wartime Walford and Naima represented Immigrant Walford.

When Andy was killed in August, while saving a little boy from an on-coming lorry, Debs was mortified because she had argued with him the last time she saw him. She gained some comfort from the fact that he had been an organ donor and his kidneys saved someone's life. In shock, Debs needed her friends on the Square to help her get over her loss and, when Colin moved into the Square, she became quite close to him. Not realizing that he was gay, Debs made a fool of herself one evening by making a drunken pass at him.

## Andy and Debbie

Early in the year Andy and Debbie's peculiar domestic set-up was complicated by having a lodger—Naima. Debbie's personal life improved when she was pursued by Det. Sgt Quick, who proposed to her in March. Having lost her job at the bank, Debbie found temporary work at the Vic, but when Andy finished his brief affair with Angie,

## Dot and Ethel

Dot went through the menopause in 1986, and suffered separate visits from her errant husband and son, who both stole from her. Ethel broke her hip and had to stay in hospital, and moved in with Dot to convalesce. This left her own flat empty and Pat Wicks quickly worked her charms on Dr Legg to become the new tenant.

## Other stories

It wasn't all gloom and doom in 1986—there were laughs as well. The carnival in April and the Glamorous Granny Contest in September were fun, and there were various less serious stories to lighten the mix. Ethel's dog Willy went missing in February, but thanks to the efforts of Det. Sgt Quick he was recovered a few weeks later.

The summer months saw another lighter story, featuring the Banned—the pop group which included Ian, Wicksy, Sharon and Kelvin. Although it spawned two hit singles in the real world, the actual story was not a great success. Somehow it lacked credibility and Julia and Tony both felt it had been an experiment that failed.

## Comings 'n' Goings 1986

The first major new character of 1986 was James Willmott-Brown (William Boyde), who appeared in March as the new area manager for Luxford and Copley, the brewery that owned the Vic. Willmott-Brown is a good example of the way minor characters can develop in EastEnders. Often a new character is introduced for a limited number of episodes, to serve a particular storyline or the story function. If the casting is good and the character 'works' on the screen, then the writers may be asked if there is potential in the character for further appearances. Another example also made her debut in 1986—Carmel Roberts (Judith Jacob). In her first appearance in June, Carmel was merely the health visitor who attended Michelle after Vicki was born. Later in the year she became a regular and moved into the Square.

Charlie Cotton (Christopher Hancock), Dot's husband, finally showed his face during March of this year and promptly stole from poor Dot before disappearing again. June 1986 saw the first appearance of Pat Wicks (Pam St Clement), and she immediately threw a spanner in the works by telling Pete that he wasn't Simon's dad.

Pat then disappeared again, only to return for good later in the year.

It's worth mentioning at this point that, of all the convoluted, confusing and mind-boggling stories that EastEnders has dealt with, the saga of the parentage of Pat's sons is the most complicated. At various times over the years the story has been amended, until the only certainty is that we will never be certain about the actual facts. For the record, the current producers believe that Pete was the father of David and may have been the father of Simon.

One of the most popular characters in the early years of the programme, and perhaps the most controversial, was Colin Russell (Michael Cashman), who was first seen on screen in August. At first the fact that he was gay was not highlighted but, by the end of the year, when barrow boy Barry Clark (Gary Hailes) moved in with him, EastEnders had a homosexual couple as regulars.

Tom Clements (Donald Tandy), a gardening rival of Arthur's at the allotment, appeared in June and quickly got a job as potman in the Vic. Dr Legg took on a locum and Dr Jaggat Singh (Amerjit Deu) arrived in November.

The biggest shock appearance of 1986 came in February, with the arrival of Den's mistress Jan (Jane How) at the Vic. Jan was originally intended to be a character who was never seen but this altered when Julia Smith changed her mind about killing Pete Beale. The original storyline was that

Colin Russell's peaceful and ordered existence was disrupted by the arrival, in his life and his flat, of young Barry Clark.

Pete would have a heart attack after the Christmas period, a shock tactic to revive interest in the show after the excitement of Christmas. When Julia decided that Pete was too useful a character to lose so early in the programme's history, Tony Holland needed to find an alternative big story—hence Jan's appearance.

As well as major characters introduced in 1986 there were numerous minor characters who appeared for the first time this year. Brad (Jonathan Stratt), the heavy from the Firm, made the first of many appearances in March. Harry Reynolds (Gareth Potter), Tessa Parker (Josephine Melville) and Eddie Hunter (Simon Henderson) joined the show for the duration of the pop group storyline and Lofty's only relative, his Auntie Irene (Katherine Parr), was seen a couple of times. Det. Sgt West (Leonard Gregory) was the latest representative of the local C.I.D. to be featured. Finally Naima's cousin Rezaul (Tanveer Ghani) was sent by her family to help in the shop.

Nick Cotton made two visits this year and Mark Fowler made three. On Mark's third visit in the summer he was accompanied by the mysterious Owen from Wales (Philip Brock), who bamboozled Arthur with his mystic musings on marrows.

There were some significant exits in 1986—the first being Det. Sgt Roy Quick (Douglas Fielding) who, spurned by Debbie Wilkins, decided to quit the force and move on. The second was also connected with Debbie as her boyfriend Andy O'Brien, the male nurse (Ross Davidson), was killed in a road accident while saving a child.

## Memorable Episodes 1986

### Episode 117 (1/4/86)

This was set against the local carnival, preparations for which had been featured over the previous few weeks. The highlight was a fancy-dress parade, which featured Pauline as Nell Gwyn, Kathy as the spirit of the sixties and Den as Dick Turpin! The episode was written by Jane Hollowood.

### Episode 133 (27/5/86)

Also written by Jane Hollowood, this episode was again dominated by one story, this time the birth of Michelle's daughter, Vicki. A great weepy cliffhanger had the proud father Den visit his new daughter to hold her just once...

### Episode 168 (25/9/86)

The entire episode, written by David Ashton, was given over to Lofty and Michelle's wedding day. In one of the best cliffhangers of the series, the episode ends as the bride arrives at the church door and hesitates...

### Episode 185 (25/11/86)

This was the third of three special episodes, written by Tony Holland and directed by Julia Smith, which took EastEnders to new territory—literally, as Den took Angie to Venice for their second honeymoon. For the first and only time in the programme's history (to date) the show was not shot entirely on videotape, as a union rule prevented Julia taking a video crew abroad and a film crew had to be used instead. Not all the foreign material was actually shot

abroad, however—the scenes in the Orient Express were recorded on a set at Elstree, with special effort being made to make the lampshades jiggle and give the impression of a train in motion.

## Episode 194 (25/12/86)

With Christmas Day falling on the Thursday, Julia was asked for an extra episode to go out on the same night. Tony Holland wrote both parts of Episode 194, the first of which went out at 6.35 p.m. and the second at 10.00 p.m. With Arthur cracking up, Den telling Angie he had filed for divorce, Pauline seeing Den give Michelle money for Vicki, and Angie and Sharon walking out of the pub in front of the punters, it was nothing if not an eventful Christmas!

The blushing bride at the wedding that never was. When it came to the crunch Michelle decided that she couldn't go through with it.

## Pick of the Year 1986

## Episode 174 (16/10/86)

The Den and Angie solo episode! It was an outrageous notion to devote an entire half-hour of drama to just two characters—unheard of in a bi-weekly serial. Once it was done, however, it set a precedent and the programme has featured two-handers and three-handers since but they will never have the impact of that first one.

Quite simply, it was a tour-de-force. Leslie Grantham and Anita Dobson, as Den and Angie, were always at their best working together rather than as separate characters, and never more so than here.

The episode was structured like a tennis match, with the poor non-speaking window-cleaner forever strolling innocently into the action. It begins with Den trying to talk to Angie to tell her that he wants to leave her and get a divorce. Angie stalls but Den persists and states his case. Angie is shocked and for a moment defeated but she then drops her bombshell and tells Den that she only has six months to live. At first Den doesn't believe her but Angie keeps to her story and, finally, her hysterical performance convinces him. He crumbles and promises to stay with her. After he leaves the room, Angie smiles in triumph.

Written by Jane Hollowood and directed by Antonia Bird, this was a classic, a half-hour television play worthy of awards. Pick of the Year and, for my money, one of the finest episodes of *EastEnders* ever.

## 1987:

# That Was the Year That . . .

After the dramatic break-up of Den and Angie's marriage at the end of the previous year, the problem facing the *EastEnders* team for 1987 was simple—how to keep the Den and Angie story going despite the couple being separated. The solution was to make the pair professional rivals and the year became dominated by the tale of two pubs; The Queen Vic and the Dagmar.

### Den and Angie spar from afar

Early in the year James Willmott-Brown left Luxford and Copley and secured the tenancy for a pub in Turpin Road, just around the corner from the Vic. At the time the Dagmar was closed and in disrepair, and the brewery which owned it, Gladstones, gave Willmott-Brown a free hand to rework the place and give it a new image. Angie immediately asked for a job as manageress and James was only too happy to have her. Throughout the spring a motley crew of workmen (Gaz, Ray, Tel and Omo), later joined by Arthur Fowler, worked to renovate the place and turn it into a modern neon and chrome wine-bar-style pub. It opened on 25 June and the competition between the two pubs began, a competition which would be played out in a number of different arenas. The first was the London In Bloom competition, in which Tom Clements for the Vic

and Arthur Fowler for the Dagmar competed to create the best decorated pub. Typically, Tom resorted to sabotage and Arthur was furious but in the end he had the last laugh as the Dagmar got a runner-up prize while the Vic got nothing. The inter-pub rivalry continued on to the sporting field with five-a-side football. Den's footballing philosophy—to win at any cost—proved to be more effective than the skilled play of the Dagmar team and the Vic won that round. As well as poaching each other's staff throughout the year, the two pubs also competed with special events, like the Dagmar's Mardi Gras night—a gay/drag evening which proved popular even with the likes of Dot and Ethel. In contrast, the Vic had a cowboy evening which pleased Pete, a big Country and Western fan, until Ian and Kelvin poked fun at the whole thing by appearing in a pantomime horse costume.

By the end of the year, however, the attraction of the Dagmar was beginning to pale for Angie—she found herself missing the Vic *and* Den. In May they received their final divorce papers and, ironically, began to get closer together again. In September Sharon arranged for them to go out one evening, and they ended up in bed together for the night.

On New Year's Eve Angie finally lost her patience with her clientele, hit Gerry the Yuppie, and walked out of the Dagmar for good. She went straight to the Vic and offered to come back—but as a business partner this time, not a wife.

A new start at a new pub? James Willmott-Brown and Angie Watts raise a glass to the future of The Dagmar, a new rival to The Queen Vic.

## The Osmans

At the café, the year began with Mehmet and Ali running the OzCabs operation—with the perennially lost OzCab 5—while Sue kept things going on the café side. When Mehmet commissioned Kathy to make a large batch of jumpers and then failed to pay for the work, Den, Pete and Tony Carpenter administered some natural justice and he left Walford. His wife, Guizin, then turned up at the café with her three kids, telling Sue that Mehmet had serious money problems and had gambled away their home. Sue and Ali took them in, and Guizin helped out in the café for a few months until Mehmet returned, having solved his money problems. Ian began working part-time at the café and Sue began to talk about wanting to move to the Isle of Dogs. This led to furious arguments with Ali and in September Sue walked out on him. In October she returned with the news that she was pregnant. On the home front, Sue and Ali had more problems when their flat was sold with them as sitting tenants. Towards the end of the year they had trouble with their new downstairs neighbour, Alan McIntyre, but when they complained they discovered that McIntyre was their new landlord!

## Naima finds love at last

At the foodstore, Naima was joined by a cousin, Rezaul, who had been sent by Naima's family to help her in the shop and to be a potential new husband. Although at first they failed to get on, they began to like each other and eventually realized that they had other plans than to marry each other. There was some friction when it appeared that Naima was interested in the new doctor, Jaggat Singh, but that was short-lived. Later in the year Naima's family sent another cousin, this time direct from India. Naima found that she liked Farrukh instantly and when he returned to India in November and asked her to marry him she quickly agreed. Rezaul returned to look after the shop for a few weeks at the end of the year, to catch poor Charlie Cotton trying to shoplift.

## The Walford Attacker

The first few months of 1987 were overshadowed by the presence of the so-called Walford Attacker, who had first made news with his assaults on women at the end of the previous year. A number of women in

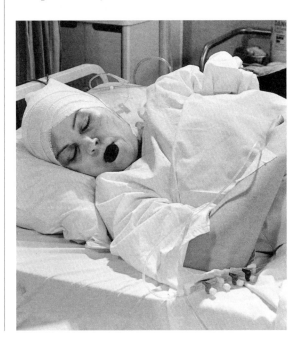

1987 saw Pat Wicks fall victim to the Walford Attacker – or did she? At first suspicion focused closer to home ...

the Square had scares late at night, including Sue and Sharon, but it was Pat Wicks who became the first victim that we knew. At the time it was not immediately clear whether Pat had been assaulted by the mysterious attacker or by someone else. There was also the possibility that the Walford Attacker was someone she knew. Pete was a prime suspect, as were Tony, Wicksy and Den. During his interview with the police Pete lost his temper and assaulted a police officer.

A few weeks later a joke played by Ian backfired when Pete turned up at the Vic for a cross-dressing party only to find that Ian had made sure that no other men were in drag. Pete stormed off, still in full make-up and wearing a dress, and later that night another woman was attacked by the Walford Attacker. Pete was later fully cleared when the real culprit was caught, while attempting to attack Debbie late one night in the launderette. This had a happy consequence as it led to Debbie becoming romantically involved with the policeman who investigated the matter, Det. Sgt Rich.

## Arthur is sent down

In the Fowler household, 1987 began with Arthur finally admitting that he had suffered a breakdown and he went into hospital. He returned to the Square in the spring to find Michelle working her fingers to the bone as a typist, earning the money to pay back the various people who were owed from the Christmas Club. Arthur faced his trial in May with a good deal of hope, the community

were seen to be behind him and Willmott-Brown helped by arranging a job for him working with the builders at the Dagmar. However, when Arthur's day in court came he was sent down for twenty-eight days. *EastEnders* had hoped to give Arthur a suspended sentence but legal research made it clear that he would have to go to prison, so scripts were amended accordingly.

Having recovered from his breakdown brought on by stealing the Christmas Club money, Arthur still had to face trial for his crime.

## A bad penny turns up again

Dot exchanged her council flat for Tom Clements' council house next door in May, which gave her more room to have Ethel stay with her. This house move happened too late for Nick's first visit of the year and so he went to stay with Colin and Barry. It transpired that Nick and Graham, Barry's elder brother, were mates—in fact, Nick had escaped prison over something which Graham had done time for. Nick then began to get Barry into all sorts of trouble and eventually Colin had to throw Nick out.

Unfortunately the story about the disruption of Colin's ordered life by the visiting Nick was slightly disrupted itself by the intrusion of real life. A strike by scene-shifters at the BBC meant that the non-permanent sets in the studio, which normally changed every week, were unable to be altered for nearly two months. This meant that Colin's flat, which should have appeared for the duration of this story, could not be seen and, when Colin finally chucked Nick out, the scene had to be played at the Vic!

Eventually the strike was resolved and normality returned, much to the relief of the script editors and writers who were amending scripts on a weekly basis to get scenes into the available sets. Nick returned later in the year at the same time as Charlie, leading to a hysterical meeting at which Dot had to introduce son to father. They had not met for years.

## Mary meets Rod

Mary continued to live a dangerous life on the verge of prostitution and got arrested at one point for soliciting. Later she was beaten up by other prostitutes and claimed at first that she had been a victim of the Walford Attacker. Mary also got into serious debt. In March, she left baby Annie 'home alone' and Dot and Ethel had to break in to rescue her. Dot contacted Mary's parents and they turned up to take the child back with them to Stockport. Mary would probably have gone into a permanent decline but for the arrival of Rod the Roadie.

Rod started living with Mary and supported her in her bid to regain Annie through the proper channels. Mary was frequently frustrated by the slow wheels of the Social Services machine but Rod kept her going. A job as cleaner at the Dagmar helped keep Mary on the straight and narrow. At the end of the year Chris Smith, Mary's father, returned to Walford with Annie, having split up with her mother. At Christmas, a drunken Chris stole a car and kidnapped Annie, planning to return to his wife. He crashed in Bridge Street and Annie spent Christmas in hospital.

## Away-days

Astute viewers of EastEnders will have noticed that some kind of away-day, an escapade out of Walford, will often happen in late June or early July and again in late October or early November. There is a practical reason—these jaunts are the result of East-Enders making a 'double-bank'. A double-bank is when an extra week's episodes of EastEnders are recorded at the same time as the regular schedule. These extra episodes, often shot mainly on location, enable the pro-

Single-mum Mary had a hard time of it when she ran away from home and found herself in Walford with her baby daughter Annie but, for a while, her relationship with Rod the Roadie gave her some real happiness and security.

duction of *EastEnders* to stop for a two-week break at Christmas.

The first double-bank of 1987 took the Walford Ladies Darts Team on a day out to Greenwich and the Isle of Dogs, while the second double-bank of 1987 was slightly different. Rather than go on location it was decided to stay at home and record the extra episodes almost exclusively on the Albert Square lot. The story for these episodes featured the visit to Walford of a TV crew making a documentary about the so-called yuppification of the East End. In the second of the two episodes the inhabitants of the Square eagerly watched their appearance on television, only to be disappointed at the way it made them all look.

## Electioneering

This year also saw the most ambitious attempt yet to make *EastEnders* feel contemporary. References to current events such as the Boat Show or Wimbledon are used to make the programmes feel up to date but these are always very general since the programme is recorded five or six weeks before transmission. When the General Election was announced in 1987 it was felt that it would be too big a national event for the programme to ignore. The problem was that the date of the election, 11 June, was only announced early in May. At that time the programmes for early June had already been made.

A clever plan was developed by Julia Smith and Tony Holland. First they cut five minutes of material from each of the four episodes in the two weeks leading up to the election. These were then replaced with specially recorded election material which was shot by Julia Smith over two extra lot recording days. Some of this material was completely new, such as representatives of each of the three major parties calling on an unimpressed Lou Beale, while other scenes were reworkings of the original scenes with added election material. Great care had to be taken to be even-handed in the treatment of each of the parties. Finally, a quick scene was recorded on the day after the election to reflect the result. The scene was then edited into the programme over the weekend and appeared on the following

September 1987 and The Queen Vic Ladies Darts team – Flights of Fancy – went on a trip to Greenwich giving Dot, Ethel and Pauline the opportunity to see the City of London from a boat on the River Thames.

The General Election 1987, and Roly demonstrates the programme's efforts to maintain complete political neutrality!

final appearances were lot scenes. This is because the lot recording for each week's episodes normally happens two weeks before the studio recording of the same episodes. This enables an actor to appear in two weeks' worth of episodes 'lot only' at the end of their contract. So that is the real explanation for Kelvin shunning his leaving party in the Vic—when the party was recorded Paul Medford was already out of contract! Paul, who had always entertained an ambition to be a singer/dancer, later enjoyed a long stage run in the hit show *Five Guys Named Moe*.

Debbie Wilkins finally left the Square in May, finding new happiness in the arms of a policeman, but this was Terry Rich rather than Roy Quick as might have been expected. Naima also left to remarry in November. A slightly less happy exit was the death of Lofty's Auntie Irene, who finally succumbed to the cancer which had been killing her slowly for years.

## Some new arrivals

Of course, there were also new faces to get to know. There were a number of new children—Mehmet's three kids, Emine, Rayif and Murat, appeared in February complete with pet snake Crush who promptly escaped, causing panic. Emine later got hurt by a thrown firework in the week of 5 November. Willmott-Brown brought his kids Luke and Sophie to visit Walford in March and Carmel's life was complicated by the arrival of her brother Darren Roberts

Tuesday. It was a complicated, difficult, last-minute operation but it did work. Nevertheless, at the next election in 1992, it was not repeated to the same extent.

## Comings 'n' Goings 1987

In 1987, more and more characters came and went, including four originals. The first of the originals to go was Tony Carpenter. His dream of a possible permanent reconciliation with Hannah dashed, Tony had briefly returned to his old trade as a silversmith, only to find his honesty compromised when he bought some dodgy silver from Nick Cotton. Finally Tony decided to return to his roots and bought himself a ticket to Trinidad.

Later in the year Kelvin also moved on, leaving Walford to begin a university course in East Anglia. As is often the case, Kelvin's

(Gary MacDonald), who came complete with his children Junior (Aaron Carrington) and baby Aisha (Aisha Jacob, playing her real mother's niece). Darren joined the programme at the same time as Rod the Roadie (Christopher McHallem) and Barry Clark's brother Graham, in a sudden influx of young men to the Square. Gary Webster, who played Graham, is now better known as Arthur Daley's nephew in *Minder*.

At the same time as these new young men appeared there was a similar batch of new young women. Tina (Eleanor Rhodes) was the young girlfriend of Ian, and she moved in with him in the basement of number 3 until her parents terminated both the arrangement and the relationship. The new woman in Den's life was Magda Czajkowski (Kathryn Apanowicz), a caterer who inspired Ian and later became involved with Wicksy. Donna (Matilda Ziegler) was the child Kathy had given birth to after her traumatic rape at the age of fourteen. Donna's appearance had been primed by the visit of her godmother earlier in the year. The godmother, June Watkins, had told Kathy that her daughter wanted to make contact but Kathy refused to see her. Donna's entrance was planned very carefully so as not to give away her secret too quickly. We established her as a compulsive liar, telling different people different versions of her past. Even so, some quick viewers still guessed the truth.

Other visitors were less complicated. The new area manager at Luxford and Copley, Mr Sparrow (Richard Ireson), proved to be as dishonest as Den and refused to take 'No'

for an answer when Den owed money. Alan McIntyre (Pip Miller), Sue and Ali's new neighbour and landlord, was an unpleasant, anti-social man who didn't care what people thought of him while Duncan Boyd (David Gillespie), the curate at the local church, had a simple honesty that appealed to the confused Sharon. Other new faces were Mary's mother, Edie Smith (Eileen O'Brien), Dagmar regular Gerry Fairweather (Jason Watkins), and Derek Taylor (Ken Sharrock), who took a shine to Pauline during the Ladies Darts Team trip to Greenwich.

Frank Butcher—perhaps the most important new character of the year—only made a brief appearance in 1987. He was Pat's old flame, her first lover. Played by Mike Reid, the casting of a comedian in a dramatic role was controversial at the time, but over the years the wisdom of that decision had been proved because Frank became one of the show's most popular characters.

## Memorable Episodes 1987

### Episode 232 (7/5/87)
This episode, written by Bill Lyons, was dominated by the trial of Arthur Fowler. A special court set had to be hired but it was too large to fit into the regular *EastEnders* studio at Elstree, Studio C, and needed an extra studio. The episode cut back and forth between the trial and the regular goings-on in the Square before climaxing with the shock decision of the Judge. Telling Arthur that, as he had betrayed people's trust he must be seen to be punished, she sentenced him to twenty-eight days.

## Episode 268 (10/9/87)

This was the second part of the Vic Ladies Darts Team's day trip to Greenwich and the Isle of Dogs, and was written by the then series script editor, John Maynard. These very funny episodes allowed Pauline an almost romantic encounter with a man called Derek Taylor who helped the group when their coach broke down. More importantly it introduced Frank Butcher, a man who would become very important for the future of EastEnders.

## Episode 300/300A (31/12/87)

With New Year's Eve falling on a Thursday, it was decided to make the now traditional extra Christmas episode for transmission on 31 December. Jane Hollowood wrote the two-parter. The second half was timed

**Ethel Skinner and Dot Cotton were the focus of Episode 248, the second EastEnders 'two-hander'.**

to go out just after half past eleven so the viewers would see the New Year in with the characters in the Vic.

## Episode 298A (25/12/87)

With the double New Year's Eve episodes already planned, the BBC threw a spanner in the works by asking for a second extra episode for Christmas Day. This would have to be written to fit between the episodes that had already been written and recorded. Jane Hollowood got the unenviable job but when the episode went out it showed no sign of its difficult origins. Featuring the aftermath of Chris Smith's drunk-driving kidnap of baby Annie, it showed what Christmas is like for children in hospital.

## Pick of the Year 1987

## Episode 248 (2/7/87)

I make no apology for picking another two-hander because this was as different from the Den and Angie episode as it could possibly be. With just the two old ladies Dot and Ethel (although, to be honest, Dot is Ethel's junior by twenty years or so) this was a beautifully written mini-play about nostalgia and growing old. Some viewers found it to be too unusual, but many others were charmed by the change of pace and the opportunity for two great actresses really to show the sadness behind the often comical characters of Dot and Ethel.

Written by Charlie Humphreys and sensitively directed by Mike Gibbon, a future producer of the show, Episode 248 is a very special episode of EastEnders. Sadly Charlie Humphreys passed away early in 1992, having written over fifty episodes of the programme, and his unique voice is much missed on Albert Square to this day.

## 1988:

# That Was the Year That . . .

There were big changes for *EastEnders* in 1988. Behind the scenes, Julia Smith took a more back-seat role as series producer, allowing Mike Gibbon as producer to take control of the day-to-day making of the programme.

On-screen, 1988 saw the end of the two-pub era as the Dagmar disappeared—in flames—in the middle of the year and was replaced by a wine bar called Strokes, operated by the local Firm of organized villains. Meanwhile it was also all change at The Queen Vic, when Pat Wicks and the Butcher family took over the tenancy.

### All change in the Square

The year began in the way it intended to go on—with change. During January, Ashraf and Sufia Karim took over in the foodstore, Ethel Skinner moved out of the Square and into sheltered housing and Barry left Colin. Over at the Vic, it had seemed that a new era was about to begin, with Den and Angie running the place as business partners. Hardly had the year started, however, than Angie was being taken off to hospital with kidney failure. This was partly due to Angie's on-going drinking problem, but the main reason had more to do with Anita Dobson and the pantomime season. Since the episodes that

Ashraf and Sufia Karim — the new owners of the shop, 'First til Last,' who came to Walford with their teenagers Shireen and Sohail.

are transmitted in late January and early February are recorded during December and early January, actors who are given leave to appear in a pantomime have to be written out for those episodes. This is why certain characters go on holiday, visit old friends or just plain disappear around that time of year.

## Heartache for Michelle and Lofty

January also saw the final collapse of Michelle's fragile marriage to Lofty. Michelle began the year in the knowledge that she was pregnant again. Pauline was delighted and told Lofty that he was to be a father. Feeling hemmed in and desperate, and already facing the trials of being a single parent to Vicki, Michelle felt that she could not cope with another child and decided to have an abortion. When Lofty found out what she had done he was angry and hurt and, in many ways, he never really recovered.

## The arrival of Kenny Beale

The Beales and the Fowlers already had problems, thanks to the arrival of Pete and Pauline's elder brother Kenny and his daughter Elizabeth from New Zealand. Inevitably the visit brought to the surface the old question of who was Wicksy's father. Pat, encouraged by the reappearance of Frank Butcher in her life, stood up to the pressure and told the Beale brothers that she didn't know which of them had fathered Simon.

## Den and Angie say goodbye

When Angie came out of hospital talk at The Queen Vic was of a fresh start and of getting a new pub elsewhere. In reality, Anita Dobson had already decided that she wanted to move on after three years in the show and the programme-makers began to plan her exit. A holiday with old friends Sonny and Ree in Spain while Angie convalesced was the first move, which allowed Angie an off-screen affair with Sonny and a plan for the new future. Sonny made the arrangements for them to begin a new life running a bar in Spain and finally, in May, Angie left for Spain while Sharon celebrated moving into a flat with her best friend Michelle, provided by Den.

Like his wife, Den had itchy feet, as did Leslie Grantham, but Julia Smith didn't want the programme to suffer the double blow of losing both Den and Angie at the same time. The solution to the problem was one of the most complex technical and creative exercises that the programme has ever attempted, and required intricate planning. The idea was to enable Den to stay as on-screen presence for an extra year while keeping Leslie Grantham working for EastEnders for only a few months.

Tony Holland and writer/story editor Bill Lyons came up with a story to put Den in prison for a year, intending that material recorded in a block of intensive filming would then be dropped into the programme for the rest of the year. The programme didn't want to make Den into a criminal, however, so he had to be put in prison for doing something that could be justified to the viewing public— otherwise there would be no sympathy for

*A visit from the exiled Kenny Beale raised long buried questions about the true identity of Simon's father...*

him. The answer lay in a storyline that was running with another character—Kathy's story.

## Trouble brews for Kathy

It was a difficult beginning of the year for Kathy, due to the whole business with Kenny; she had to be very patient and supportive of Pete while the sordid history of Wicksy's parentage was investigated. Kathy was then asked to leave her volunteer job with the Samaritans after an alleged breach of confidence. In April, Donna finally revealed her true identity to Kathy and was disappointed when Kathy rejected her again. Willmott-Brown, who had now moved into the flat above his pub, was able to offer some good news for Kathy and gave her a job as a barmaid at the Dagmar. This proved to be a fresh source of friction between Pete and Kathy—he didn't like the pub, the clientele or the clothes Kathy felt she had to wear to look good at work. Things were not helped by Willmott-Brown's evident and growing interest in Kathy as he bought her presents and confided in her about the break-up of his own marriage.

Meanwhile, Den had moved out of the Vic and into the wine bar in Turpin Road, which had been purchased by the Firm to use the basement for illegal gambling. Den was needed to secure a licence to sell alcohol but it soon became clear that the real boss at Strokes, as the wine bar was renamed, was the mysterious Joanne.

With all the pieces in place, the climax came in July. While Wicksy planned a birthday party at the estate flat, Kathy made arrangements to stay at the Fowlers for the night. Pete was away, driving Lou to Leigh-on-Sea for a much-needed break—Lou had been feeling very ill for some time. That night Willmott-Brown asked Kathy to stay after work for a drink. The situation got out of hand and what began as seduction ended as rape. Den discovered Kathy and, after getting her to a place of safety, he sought out his Firm contacts, Joanne and Brad, and demanded that something should be done to sort out Willmott-Brown. When Joanne failed to get authorization to do anything immediately, Den persuaded Brad to use some initiative and do something himself. Later, Den watched with pleasure as a fire-bomb was thrown into the deserted Dagmar and it exploded into flames.

## Den does the decent thing

Unfortunately the net result of this enterprise was to attract more police attention into the area than the Firm could feel comfortable with. Joanne and her colleague, the sinister Mr Mantel, made it quite clear to Den that he would be expected to take the rap for the arson to take the heat off the area. He was even offered a salary—£20 000 for every year he would spend inside.

After a little thought, Den decided that a better option was to let the police think he was guilty and go on the run. The Firm agreed to his revised plan and Den said his goodbyes and was taken off to a safe house, where he was looked after by Christine, an employee of the Firm who Den swiftly

Happy smiles for James Willmott-Brown and Kathy Beale give no sign that James will soon rape his favourite barmaid . . .

seduced. The safe house was, in fact, a rather nice house in a leafy avenue in Hatch End, North West London. When it became clear that the Firm had decided that the best Den Watts was a dead Den Watts, Den escaped and visited an old friend in Manchester (again, the real location was much closer to Borehamwood). He finally gave himself up to the police, hoping to force the Firm into honouring their original deal.

Den was remanded in Dickens Hill Prison in September. For the next five months he was seen, in the company of a small group of new characters also confined at the prison, on a regular basis in *EastEnders*. This material was shot in one intensive burst of activity in less than a month at Dartmoor Prison, Devon, and was written at an equal pace by Tony Holland and Bill Lyons. When these segments were written and recorded, they were done entirely in isolation and in advance—the production team had no real idea of the other material that would have to fit around them in each episode. That meant the storylining of the programme had to slot neatly around the Dickens Hill material that had been recorded for each episode. It proved to be a major headache at times!

**Other storylines**

Although the Dickens Hill, soap-within-a-soap, dominated the second half of the year it was not the only major storyline of 1988. There was the new regime at The Queen Vic, with Frank Butcher and Pat Wicks securing the tenancy of the pub, after a fair bit of bribing Sparrow, the brewery area

manager. Once Frank was installed in the Vic, his teenage kids, Diane and Ricky, came to live in the Square, and Ricky became interested in Shireen the Karims' daughter, for a while.

Barry became involved in a mobile disco business with Ian and Darren, and the two lads soon decided to go it alone and bought Darren out. Darren, whose varied business interests had already seen him putting on a porn video and strip show at the Community Centre, neglected to tell them that the equipment was only on HP and the disco promptly folded when the gear was repossessed. Darren did a runner, leaving Carmel and her new white boyfriend, Matthew, to look after his kids, Junior and Aisha.

Changes at the surgery saw Dr Legg's nephew, David, joining him in the practice and Michelle began working as the surgery receptionist. Dot, Ethel and Ethel's new 'boyfriend', Benny Bloom, became involved in forming a Neighbourhood Watch for Albert Square. Arthur spent a happy few months working for the Karims at the foodstore before losing his job, again.

Colin found new love with a man called Guido Smith, who he met through his work. Colin also had a health scare during the autumn and for a moment it looked like *EastEnders* might be about to do an Aids story. In fact this was never the idea—it was felt that the most simplistic and unhelpful 'message' that the programme could give out would be to have its only homosexual character become HIV positive.

Before he went, Den gave Wicksy some words of wisdom on how to deal with

A day out at the zoo for Matthew, Carmel and her nephew and niece Junior and Aisha.

women. Basically, his advice was to 'love 'em and leave 'em', and Wicksy put this into practice, playing off Mags, Donna and Cindy against each other. Later in the year this proved his undoing, as Cindy became more impressed with Ian's drive and ambition than with Wicksy's shiftless indifference. Here *EastEnders* was sowing the seeds of a situation that would provide much story material for many years to come...

## Comings 'n' Goings 1988

Four more of the originals left the programme in 1988; Mary, Lou, Lofty and Angie. Mary had been one of the most striking of the original characters, a lone mother with a small baby, who hid herself under punk make-up, was unable to read or write and was a Northerner alone in a southern city. She left Walford the way she arrived, running away from her parents. Lou was frequently ill during 1988, and after a rest in Leigh-on-Sea she returned to Walford

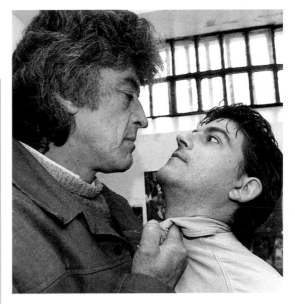

in July in time to die. Lofty, heart-broken after Michelle aborted their child, moved on to become a handyman in a children's home and Angie found new love in the arms of Sonny and left England to run a bar in Spain.

Other exits during the year included poor old Tom Clements, potman and gardener, who died after suffering a stroke in The Queen Vic. Barry Clark left Walford to work on a cruise ship and Chris Smith left after his company ran into financial problems and had to be bought out by Walford Investments, the Firm's money-lending arm. Magda Czajkowski (Mags), let down by Wicksy and Den, took her Symphony Foods catering business to pastures new and Darren, proving that discretion is the better part of valour, did a runner when his various activities got a little too hot to handle.

Among the visitors were Kenny Beale (Michael Attwell) and his daughter Elizabeth (Lucy Bayler) from New Zealand, who arrived in the spring. Also making an appearance was Brian Wicks (Leslie Schofield), Pat's *other* ex-husband and, according to Pat in the middle of the year, the real father of Simon. New youngsters in this year included Sohail (Ronnie Jhutti) and Shireen Karim (Nisha Kapur), Ricky (Sid Owen) and Diane Butcher (Sophie Lawrence), and Junior's little girlfriend Melody (Lyanne Compton). A major batch of new characters was needed for the Den/prison storyline. In Walford these included Joanne (Pamela Salem), the manager of Strokes; Mr Mantel (Pavel Douglas) of Walford Investments; Brad (Jonathan Stratt), the Firm's local thug (who had appeared before but never so often as

during this storyline); and Det. Insp. Ashley (Robin Lermitte) who joined Walford C.I.D.

Left: Prison and Barnsey has a quiet word with Nick. Right: Albert and Lou Beale (Gary Olson and Karen Meagher) in 'Civvy Street'.

determined to close down the Firm. Inside Dickens Hill, Den was joined by prison officers Crane (Raymond Trickett) and Stone (Jeremy Young), and fellow prisoners Barnsey (John Hallam), Queenie (John Labanowski), Vic (Michael Brogun) and Brownlow (David James), and the more familiar faces of Johnny Harris (Michael O'Hagan) and Nick Cotton (John Altman).

Back in Walford, the Butcher family was completed by the arrival of Frank's mother Mo Butcher (Edna Doré), and Carmel gained a new partner, a white man called Matthew Jackson (Steven Hartley). Perhaps the most important character for the future had a very low-key entrance, appearing as another market-trader at first but quickly becoming involved with both Wicksy and Ian. This was Cindy Williams (Michelle Collins), who initially appeared helping her mother run a hat stall in Turpin Road.

## Memorable Episodes 1988

### Civvy Street (22/12/88)

Although not actually an episode of *EastEnders*, special mention should be made of the extra Christmas episode screened this year. It was a one-off programme called 'Civvy Street' which told the story of the Square during the Second World War. Written by Tony Holland and directed by Julia Smith, this special episode filled in some of the background to the *EastEnders* characters and was a charming experiment. It was not the easiest of projects to write, however—Tony Holland was most upset to discover that Dot had been too young during the war to be featured as a useful character and also complained that the major events of the war occurred in the wrong order for effective drama!

### Episode 306 (21/1/88)

This was the episode in which Michelle had her abortion, which was paid for by Den. Tony McHale was the writer. Ironically, and purely by coincidence, the episode was screened the same day that a Private Member's Bill was discussed in the House of Commons which sought to reduce the number of weeks following conception in which an abortion can be carried out.

### Episode 316 (25/2/88)

Also by Tony McHale, this was another corker, with the long-awaited show-down between Pat, Kenny and Pete over the parentage of Wicksy. At this stage Pat said that either of the brothers could be the boy's father—but there was also a strong hint that the real father might have been Den!

### Episode 350 (23/6/88)

In this episode, written by Gerry Huxham, Den opened his new wine bar, Strokes. Den, in a white tuxedo, conjured up visions of Humphrey Bogart in *Casablanca* and, inevitably, at one point he instructed his pianist to 'play it again'.

### Episode 355 (12/7/88)

This was the second of three episodes written by Tony McHale which covered the rape of Kathy, and they were all examples of *EastEnders* at its best. This episode received a good deal of criticism for showing the police as unsympathetic and unhelpful to a rape victim. The story, however, continued in the next episode, when Kathy reached the police station and received very sympathetic treatment from a male detective and a W.P.C. Tony McHale had researched the subject in depth with the police and was determined to portray the broad range of ways that the police dealt with the serious subject of rape. A senior woman police officer later congratulated the programme on its even-handed and honest portrayal of the incident.

A new venture for Den Watts – Strokes Wine Bar – but it was the Firm's Joanne who really called the shots here, not Den.

## Pick of the Year 1988

### Episode 359 (28/7/88)

This was written by Tony Holland and directed by Julia Smith. The previous two episodes (358 and 358A), also by Tony Holland, had featured the return of Lou from Leigh-on-Sea, intent on sorting things out with her family. She spent the two episodes arranging her affairs, seeing various members of her family, passing on advice and giving them presents. At the end of the second episode she announced 'That's you lot sorted out. I can go now.'

At the start of Episode 359 Lou was found to have died peacefully in her sleep. The episode then jumped to a few days later and the day of her funeral. An emotional episode, which featured Pete breaking down at the graveside, it ended with Pete proposing a toast in the Vic to absent friends and that 'bloody old bag'. The episode is also notable for featuring, for the first and only time (to date), a train crossing the railway viaduct in Bridge Street. This was a special effects shot commissioned especially for the occasion.

Lou Beale's funeral. Sharon's boyfriend Duncan, conducted the service.

# 1989:

# That Was the Year That . . .

For *EastEnders*, 1989 was a funny year—in more ways than one. It was a transitional year with another three of the original characters leaving, along with half a dozen other regulars.

## Off-screen changes

It was also a year of change behind the scenes as original production designer, Keith Harris, left the show. Co-creators Julia Smith and Tony Holland had both decided that the time had come for them to move on to other things as well, and their final contribution to the programme coincided with Den's exit in February. Without their hands to guide the programme, the new producer Mike Gibbon turned to the most experienced of the writers to take over the task of storylining the programme, so Charlie Humphreys, Jane Hollowood and Tony McHale shared this job for much of the year.

There was a deliberate effort to increase the lighter, more comic, aspects of life in the Square. By this stage in the programme's history it had earned its long-standing reputation for being unrelenting doom and gloom and the programme-makers were determined to change this. That led to the introduction of some characters who were deliberately conceived as 'comic' characters. In many ways this was a brave experiment

and the results were entertaining, but many viewers felt that this period of *EastEnders* lacked a certain edge. In reality, looking back at the stories that were covered during the year, that analysis doesn't really hold water because issues like domestic violence, drugs, rape, homoeopathic medicine and racism were all featured. Perhaps it was the new emphasis on a more balanced mix between light and heavy storylines that gave the illusion that the show had lost something.

Popular television had also been given a boost by the introduction in July of the previous year of the twice-weekly version of *The Bill*, a hard-hitting, gritty slice of police life drama which seemed to be challenging *EastEnders* in providing a realistic vision of modern life in London. So perhaps it was understandable that at the end of the year Peter Cregeen, the new Head of Series at the BBC, poached Michael Ferguson who had been a producer on *The Bill* to become executive producer of *EastEnders*.

## Life carries on in Albert Square

Despite all this, it was for the changes on-screen that the viewers will remember 1989. The first two months saw the climax to the Dickens Hill story, as one by one the storylines of the other characters were concluded, until the date of Den's trial approached. The Firm made another effort to get to Den in order to keep him quiet, but Den managed to escape from Brad and made a rendezvous with Michelle at the 'usual place'. Unfortunately Michelle was followed by the Firm's assassin, and after she left Den he was shot.

It was a year of new businesses in the Square, almost as if Walford itself was making a fresh start. Ian Beale took over the café and began his development into the sharp-minded businessman we know and loathe today; Frank Butcher returned to his original game and opened up a car lot on the site of Chris Smith's failed haulage company; Julie Cooper arrived from the North to open a hairdressing salon in Turpin Road; and Frank and Pat bought up the

Would you buy a used car from this man? Meet Frank Butcher — always ready to make you a deal.

Bed and Breakfast on the far side of the Square to add to their portfolio of other interests.

Some of the main stories in this year were ramifications of past events already seen in *EastEnders*. Now that the programme had built up an on-screen history, more and more events became self-generating, as stories spawned sequels and follow-ups.

Julie Copper (centre) opens her hairdressing salon in Turpin Road, aided by her staff Marie and Michelle.

## Pete and Kathy split up

The previous year had ended with Pete becoming depressed and despondent about the state of his marriage. So 1989 began with his appearance in court for drunk-driving, for which he lost his licence. Meanwhile Kathy was being hassled by Willmott-Brown to drop the rape charge. With Ian's help Kathy set up Willmott-Brown and he was arrested.

Kathy finally told Pete that their marriage

was over in January and she left the Square. Pete went into an immediate decline and, a month later and drinking heavily again, he stole Mehmet's car, vowing to kill Willmott-Brown who he blamed for all his unhappiness. Pete crashed into another car and injured the passenger. Kathy returned later in the year and began renting Kelvin's flat. At the end of April she faced the trauma of reliving the rape for the trial of Willmott-Brown and was relieved when he was found guilty and sent to prison for three years.

At the end of August Pete's luck improved when he won £1000 on the Premium Bonds. After another court appearance, this time for his second drunk-driving offence, Pete was given a three-month suspended sentence and banned from driving for five years. To cheer himself up, he decided to take a long holiday to New Zealand to see his brother Kenny. When he returned he found that Laurie Bates had arrived in Walford, taken over the hat stall and begun to sell fruit and veg in direct competition with the Fowler/Beale stall. This story, known as the 'Great Fruit 'n' Veg War' in the script department, gave a new impetus to Pete, and took the character in a new direction.

## Eternal triangles

This was also the year of love triangles—there was not only the Pete–Kathy–Laurie trio but also Cindy caught between her engagement to Ian and her love for Wicksy (who started living with Sharon in the late

A challenge to Pete Beale — a new fruit and veg man arrives on the market — Laurie Bates. And to make matters worse, he became involved with Pete's ex, Kath!

summer); Paul Priestley, who was tempted by the older woman Julie Cooper (much to the disgust of his girl-friend, Diane); and Sufia Karim, suffering over her husband Ashraf's affair with Stella.

## Some important issues

As ever, there were also the big 'issue' stories. For the first time the programme told a complete drugs story, with the sad tale of Donna's descent into heroin addiction. Matilda Ziegler's performance gave the story credibility and the final death scenes were the most powerful anti-drugs images ever screened in the programme.

The programme also dealt with the issue of domestic violence for the first time, with the break-up of Carmel and Matthew's marriage. Another story involved Pauline ignoring a health problem she had, and trying to use homoeopathic remedies rather than seek medical help. In the end her fibroids were discovered by chance after Ricky knocked her over in his Mini, and Pauline spent Christmas in hospital.

## Some lighter moments

Humour was an important element in the storylines during 1989, with a greater amount of slapstick and light comedy than in previous years. The credibility of the programme was stretched, perhaps, by some of the stories, such as Arthur's unlikely success on the fictional TV game show *Cat and Mouse*. Behind the scenes we had a lot of fun trying to work out the rules to the game show and, in wild moments of fantasy, we even wondered if any television company

would want to make *Cat and Mouse*, but as yet no enquiries have been received!

Other stories were also handled in a lighter manner. Mo Butcher's involvement with the Community Centre and her battles with the wheelchair-bound council officer Mr Rhodes were essentially humorous, as were the escapades of the local Brownie

Who says *EastEnders* is all doom and gloom? One of the programme's funniest episodes saw Arthur appear on a TV quiz show.

pack under Marge Green, who was Brown Owl. Mo took her place and took charge. The story may have been intended to be fun but references to Brownies behaving badly caused great offence to the Brownie movement, and an official complaint was made and upheld. The BBC had to make a public apology for the misrepresentation of the movement. It was a salutary lesson to those of us in the script department to be very vigilant in ensuring, as far as possible, that no group or individual was offended by an unintentional slight in a script.

The year also saw two weddings, which couldn't have been more different from each other. The first was Pat and Frank's and was celebrated in style with a street party reception. The second was Ian and Cindy's, which took place in a register office, with the bride very obviously pregnant.

## Comings 'n' Goings 1989

The pace of comings and goings was fast and furious during 1989, as the programme tried to find a new direction. More originals departed, and 1989 finally saw the end of Den, as he fell victim to the Firm's gunman.

## The sad story of the Osmans

Sue and Ali also left during this year, both in sad circumstances. Their marriage, always volatile, broke up in March when drug addict Donna told Sue that she had been sleeping with Ali. When Ali's brother Mehmet comforted Sue, Ali believed she had been having an affair with him and he threw her out of the flat. After taking legal advice Sue took baby Ali and disappeared. In May,

Ali tracked her down and found her visiting Hassan's grave. There he kidnapped the baby, causing Sue to suffer a mental breakdown and be admitted to a mental hospital. For a few months Ali tried to make it on his own, looking after baby Ali and working for Frank on his car lot, but he soon

returned to his gambling ways. In October, after making the fatal mistake of losing at cards to his landlord McIntyre, Ali left the Square, evicted from his flat and having lost the café to Ian. The year also saw the last of Mehmet and Guizin, who returned to Cyprus in the middle of another marital break-up.

An *EastEnders* tragedy, the sad case of Donna Ludlow, Kathy's daughter, conceived when Kathy was raped as a teenager.

## Drama in the Square

Other exits were more dramatic—Donna choking on her own vomit in Dot's sitting room after an overdose of heroin was especially gruesome. Carmel's marriage began to go wrong when Matthew proved to have an ugly and combustible temper. After a particularly violent incident ended with Junior using a knife to protect his aunt, it became clear that something had to be done. A month after Carmel threw Matthew out of the flat her father died and she left the Square to live with her sister. At the start of the year, Colin Russell finally learned that he had multiple sclerosis and decided to go and live with his brother in Bristol. As luck would have it, time pressure on one episode during February led to a scene being cut which explained why Guido also decided to move on, rather than stay in Walford. Unfortunately, without that scene, no explanation was ever given for Guido's disappearance and fans were still asking about him months later. When Ian and Cindy moved into the flat some time later, many viewers expected them to find a starving Guido still in there!

Off-screen, Ethel's boyfriend Benny Bloom was reported to have died and actor Arnold Yarrow, who had left the series by the time of his character's death, had to reassure his friends and family that *he* was still very much alive. In fact, Arnold went on to join the *EastEnders* script team in 1992. Legg's nephew, David Samuels, also left during the year. He returned to Israel to marry his girlfriend, Ruth, leaving the old doctor alone in his Walford practice.

## A few new faces

The summer saw a group of new characters who all joined at around the same time. The first of these was Marge Green (Pat Coombs), the retiring Brown Owl, who worked for the mysterious Doris at the Bed and Breakfast. When Frank and Pat took over the business they inherited Marge's services too. Marge was a well-meaning, slightly batty older lady, who worked well in partnership with the much tougher Mo Butcher.

Other newcomers included brassy Northerner Julie Cooper (Louise Plowright) who opened a hairdressing salon; odd-job man Paul Priestley (Mark Thrippleton); and Trevor Short (Phil McDermott), Paul's mate and the nearest thing to a village idiot that Walford has seen for many a long year.

March saw the arrival of Hazel, who tried to convince Dot that her sister's baby was her own and had been fathered by Nick. After Charlie managed to unveil her scam she disappeared but the programme-makers were sufficiently impressed with actress Virginia Fiol to bring the character back later in the year as a potential partner for Rod.

Michelle found new love in the shape of Danny Whiting (Saul Jephcott), a computer salesman who she met through her work at the surgery, but he was married with three children and it was clear that the relationship wouldn't last. However, Michelle couldn't put Danny out of her mind and they got back together again later in the year, with her accepting the role as 'the other woman'.

Laurie Bates (Gary Powell) came to Turpin Road Market to set up a rival fruit and veg stall to Pete's. His rivalry went further when

he began to get interested in Pete's estranged wife, Kathy.

Other new arrivals included Marie (Vicky Murdock), who joined owner Julie and Michelle as the third member of staff at the hairdressing salon; Mr Rhodes (Sid Williams), a council official who happened to be a paraplegic and had a running battle with Mo Butcher about the way the Community Centre was run; and Stella (Cindy O'Callagan), Ashraf Karim's white mistress. Vince Johnson (Hepburn Graham), a friend of Darren's, arrived in Walford bringing money for Junior from his missing dad, and Pete's holiday romance girlfriend Barbara (Alannah O'Sullivan) flew in from New Zealand to join Pete for the Christmas festivities in Albert Square.

Marge Green and Frank's mum Mo Butcher – not the most effective leaders Walford's Brownies have ever had ...

**EastEnders**

THE FIRST 10 YEARS

A meeting with destiny
on the local canal bank for
Den Watts, as an assassin
lurks ...

## Memorable Episodes 1989

### Episode 418 (23/2/89)

*EastEnders* returned to the stretch of the Grand Union Canal at Alperton in North London for a final meeting between Den and Michelle. The episode ended with Den being shot and falling into the canal. The scene where Den actually hit the water had to be taped at the BBC's Ealing Film Studios, using a water tank, because it wasn't safe to have Leslie Grantham fall into the less than healthy waters of the Grand Union Canal. When the episode was finished, however, Jonathan Powell, Controller of BBC1, requested that this final shot should be removed, to allow for the possibility of Den returning at a later date. In protest, writer Tony Holland and director Julia Smith had their names taken off the credits.

### Episode 432 (13/4/89)

This was a half-hour mini-tragedy, written by Charlie Humphreys, with Donna, rejected by Kathy, overdosing on heroin. Dot, who realized that the girl needed help, went to fetch Carmel, but her continuing story of domestic violence meant that Carmel was unable to visit Donna. By the time Dot found out, it was too late, Donna had been left alone too long and was lying on the carpet, dead.

### Episode 446 (1/6/89)

Written by Tony McHale, this was one of the funniest and most outrageous episodes

of *EastEnders* to date. Featuring Arthur's appearance on the live quiz show *Cat and Mouse* it could easily have drifted into situation comedy but Tony McHale kept the episode balanced with the more realistic drama back in the Square, with Cindy causing an argument between Ian and Wicksy, and Frank proposing to Pat.

## Episode 452 (22/6/89)

New writer Tony Jordan was given the task of writing the two very different weddings

of the year. The first was the wedding of Frank and Pat, celebrated with a street party organized by Mo. Although planned for a summer's day, the lot material was recorded in the middle of almost gale-force winds! Tony had fun by writing in a character, who never spoke, who had managed to join the Albert Square wedding festivities even though he didn't know any of the wedding party!

A windy wedding day for Pat and Frank, here enjoying a street party reception with Sharon and Wicksy who, at the time, were partners themselves.

## Episode 484 (12/10/89)

The second of Tony Jordan's 1989 wedding episodes, this was a less cheerful affair: Ian and Cindy's wedding in a local register office. In fact, the register office was the producer's Elstree office, which had recently been redecorated. The happy day ended in tears, however, with Cindy rowing with her new father-in-law and Ian arguing with his new wife. Best man Wicksy, who knew one of the reasons for Cindy's unhappiness— that she was carrying his baby—could only stand and watch.

## Pick of the Year 1989

### Episode 429 (4/4/89)

Once again I have chosen an episode with only two characters in it. This was the third two-hander, and featured Sharon and Michelle. Written by Tony McHale, it returned to the model established by the first Den and Angie solo episode, with revelations and major changes to an important relationship. Here, in the aftermath of Den's death, the two friends start an evening at home with a bottle of wine and their memories. Sharon begins to speculate about the identity of the mysterious woman that the police reported as having been seen with Den not long before his death. When Sharon tells Michelle that she feels that she and Vicki are her family now, Michelle is able to tell her the truth—that Den was Vicki's father. It

soon becomes clear that this was a mistake as Sharon takes the news very badly, feeling hurt, angry and deceived. She leaves the flat wishing that Michelle had never told her. Things would never be quite the same between them.

This episode gave Letitia Dean and Susan Tully the chance to demonstrate just how much they had grown up as actresses during the four years they had been in the programme, and both gave superlative performances. Directed by producer Mike Gibbon, this had to be the outstanding episode of the year.

A very different wedding: Cindy Williams — already pregnant with Wicksy's son — marries Ian Beale.

Happy flatmates Michelle and Sharon before they fall out when Michelle reveals the indentity of Vicki's dad — Den Watts

# That Was the Year That . . .

Behind the scenes, 1990 was a year of great change for *EastEnders*. Michael Ferguson, as executive producer, introduced a system of having two producers responsible for the making of each alternate pair of episodes, and Richard Bramall and Corinne Hollingworth were the first of these new producers. In addition, Michael changed the way stories were found, by asking for all stories to be written as complete narratives, with beginnings, middles and ends, before they were broken down into precise episodes for the scriptwriters. These stories were to come from any of the writers, the producers or from the expanded script department, which now had two story editors (senior script editors) and a storyline editor, in addition to script editors working on individual scripts.

The new system led to some very strong, intense story-telling. Another innovation that Michael Ferguson introduced was a far greater amount of location work than had previously been the norm. Now *EastEnders* would have the opportunity on a regular basis, to move away from the Square to tell its stories. It was a challenging period, both for those who had worked on the show for some time and for the many new faces that appeared at Elstree, but the results on the screen were a programme with a new sense of vitality, and a programme more in touch with the real world than it had been for a while.

## Diane does a bunk

One story that dominated the beginning of the year was the effect on the Butcher household of Diane running away from home. Diane had felt unhappy for many months and the decision of her boyfriend, Paul Priestley, to leave Walford just before Christmas didn't help. When it seemed that her family had forgotten her birthday, although in fact they were preparing a surprise birthday party for her, it proved to be too much for Diane and she defiantly walked off into the night. For weeks a frantic Frank searched, without success, for his missing daughter.

> Diane Butcher whose three months homeless on the streets of London were revealed in two special episodes of *EastEnders* in March 1990.

When it was originally storylined, the story was open-ended and we were not sure if Diane would ever be found. One of Michael Ferguson's first decisions was that she *must* be found, and the subsequent story of her coming home and adjusting to life back in Walford was developed. One of the side effects of her time on the streets was her involvement with artist/photographer Matthew Taylor, which sparked off Diane's own emerging interest in art. Later in the year this was demonstrated when Diane painted a mural on the side of the Butcher house.

## The final farewell to Den

The discovery of one of Den's rings on a market stall led to the canal being dredged in April, and a body being found. The new

team, plagued by constant enquiries from viewers and journalists about the possibility of Dirty Den returning to the programme, had decided to bury the matter (if you'll excuse the phrase) once and for all. In May, Den Watts was finally buried, and Sharon began a search for her natural birth parents.

## Nick's new scam
Nick Cotton returned in an outrageous story in which he tried to poison his mother while claiming to be a born-again Christian. In March Dot won £1000 through the *Gazette* Bingo game and no sooner had the news been reported in the paper than Nick was back. This time, he assured her, things were different, now that he too had found salvation in God. With the help of a bogus priest called Alistair, Nick managed to convince his mother of his new-found faith and then began a slow campaign to control her eating habits and poison her. At first it was not clear if Nick was genuinely concerned about Dot or not, but as the weeks passed it became obvious that he did intend to kill his mum, as we saw him practising a suicide note in Dot's handwriting. The arrival of Charlie complicated matters for Nick, but despite his father's interference and that of Ethel, Nick pressed on. At the last moment, however, Dot seemed to realize what was happening, and agreed to eat the special meal Nick had prepared for her. Whether Nick felt guilty or just couldn't go through with it once his victim knew what was happening to her we will never know, but he stopped her eating the meal and left. Once again Dot was left alone, broken-hearted at what her own son had been prepared to do to her.

## Problems for the market
A more public battle featured during the summer as the market's future was threatened by a possible development along Turpin Road. Pete and the other traders fought a long campaign to save their market but the solution came through other means. Michelle did some temping for the local council after Julie's hairdressing salon closed down, and her boss, Stuart Kendle, tried to bribe Pete into dropping his opposition to the new development. Newcomers Phil and Grant Mitchell, impressed by Pete's bottle in standing up to the council (to the point of having his stall demolished by a JCB) broke into the council offices and stole the evidence that proved Kendle was corrupt. After Michelle took the information to the Borough Surveyor the development plans were shelved and the market was saved.

## Love hurts
The big story of the year was the latest version of the eternal triangle between Wicksy, Cindy and Ian. In January, Cindy and newborn baby Steven came out of hospital and back to the Square. On the night of their return Wicksy made an excuse to meet Cindy secretly in the middle of the Square and told her that he wanted her and their baby. Their conversation was overheard, and a couple of episodes later Michelle was revealed as the accidental eaves-

Time for Den's little princess to grow up – Sharon Watts says her final goodbyes to her late father at his funeral.

dropper. This put her in a difficult position, as Wicksy and Sharon were still together at the time.

By May, Frank and Pat had decided to give up the tenancy of the Vic, which Sharon and Wicksy were managing for them. Sharon and Wicksy planned to apply for the tenancy themselves but Sharon became angered by Wicksy's lack of commitment to the idea. At the same time Wicksy was becoming obsessed with Cindy. By the time the couple's application had been rejected by the brewery in June, their relationship had dissolved. In July Wicksy moved out of Walford to live in a bedsit elsewhere in London, while Cindy tried to convince her mother-in-law Kathy that she had no intention of leaving Ian. Kathy had reason to doubt that—having overheard Cindy trying to persuade Wicksy to stay one night when babysitting.

With Wicksy out of the picture, Cindy realized that she did want to be with him after all and began visiting him in his bedsit. At the start of August she told Ian the truth— that she was in love with another man and that Steven was not his son. In a fury, Ian drove off and deliberately crashed his van, perhaps in an attempt to kill himself. Ian temporarily lost his memory and, while he lay in hospital recovering, Cindy persuaded Wicksy to move into the flat with her. She then took the opportunity to escape for a few weeks to house-sit for her parents in Devon. Wicksy joined her there and then Ian arrived, newly-released from hospital.

Stunt work is rare in *EastEnders* but when there is a stunt it's always spectacular. Here Ian turns his van over ..

first getting Wicksy sacked from the Vic and then offering him work as a waiter—but only so he could set him up to look like a thief. Finally, at Christmas, Ian tampered with the brakes of his van before Wicksy was due to use it for a job. Seeing Wicksy about to take Steven with him, Ian intervened and ended up travelling with Wicksy himself. After the inevitable accident, when it became clear to Wicksy that Ian had been responsible, Wicksy decided that he and Cindy had to leave Walford and they did.

## Sharon looks for her natural parents

In the middle of all this, Sharon had begun a search for her natural parents and, using Cindy as a confidante, she tracked down Carol, her birth mother, in August. At their first meeting things were awkward, but they continued to see each other for a while. Later it became clear that Carol was interested in Sharon as a friend rather than as a daughter and Sharon decided to stop seeing her, realizing that to all intents and purposes Den and Angie had been her real parents.

## More worries for the Butchers

A sadder story featured more pressure for Frank and Pat Butcher as Mo began to show signs of ageing. At first it was just forgetfulness—a bath left running, or a pint of milk put in the oven rather than the fridge—but later it became more serious. After tests Frank was told that Mo was suffering from dementia. In October she accidentally started a fire in her flat and had to come to live at the B and B. After that her deterioration was rapid. In a lucid moment she wrote Frank a

There he learned that Wicksy was the other man—a revelation that totally pole-axed him. | **Cindy spent a few idyllic days with the father of her son at her parents' house in Devon, but the happiness couldn't last.**

Back in Walford he destroyed all traces of Cindy in the flat and set about rebuilding his life.

When Cindy and Wicksy returned a week later the story had become public and a cold war developed between the Butchers, who put Cindy and Wicksy up in the Bed and Breakfast, and the Fowlers/Beales. In October Ian arranged blood tests and learned that he could not be Steven's father. He abandoned his plans to seek custody and threw himself into building up a travelling catering business, which he roped Sharon into. Ian then started a campaign of revenge,

letter asking him not to let her end up like her grandmother who had gone dotty and that she would prefer to die than suffer the same fate.

## Cupid causes trouble

In the Karim household, Shireen was dreading the arranged marriage that her father was setting up for her but when she met Jabbar, her prospective husband, she was delighted to find that she rather liked him. Sadly, Ashraf upset the apple cart when the boy's family learnt that Ashraf was still involved in his long-running affair with his white mistress, Stella, and they called off the marriage.

Ricky Butcher, who had found himself work as a mechanic at the Mitchell brothers' garage, got into trouble with his bosses when he started going out with their younger sister Samantha.

## The Mitchells start as they mean to go on

The Mitchell brothers were also bad news for the Fowlers when Arthur got a job delivering things for Phil. When Mark took a delivery for his father, to help out, he was arrested— the package he was carrying contained forged MOT certificates. After pressure from Michelle, who told Phil about her father's breakdown over the Christmas Club money, Phil went to the police and took the blame. Still feeling guilty, Phil later suggested that Arthur should set himself up as a gardener and provided him with a van and a phone to get the business going.

## Ian ages fast!

The year saw a deliberate continuity 'error' when Ian celebrated his twenty-first birthday just two years after his eighteenth! The producers felt that Ian needed to be a bit older if they were to tell the stories that they wanted to run for him later in the year.

Grant and Phil Mitchell were designed to make life in Albert Square a touch livelier — a brief they soon fulfilled!

## Comings 'n' Goings 1990

Early in 1990 a number of characters left as the new production machine cleared the way for new characters and a new direction.

### A few departures from the Square

In February Marge left, conned by her cousin Fred into becoming his mother's companion on a cruise. Veteran comedy actress Pat Coombs was upset to be leaving the programme so soon, but sadly there was no place in the new plan for a character whose prime function was to be comic relief. Marge's departure was followed by Danny's, the two-timing rat who invited Michelle to join him in a new life in Newcastle even as he was trying to make amends with his wife. Michelle decided to stay in Walford and sent him packing, and a week later she met Danny's wife and discovered the real extent of his duplicity.

Paul Priestley had left to return to the North before Christmas 1989, one of the many factors that led to Diane Butcher running away from home at the start of the year. Paul returned in February but was unable to help Frank in his search for Diane. Paul then made his final exit, taking dozy old Trevor with him. Drifters Hazel and Rod gave up their short-lived occupation of Colin's flat and went off to see the world.

Rod's last act was to sell some African statues to Frank, who then sold them to Vince Johnson for a fraction of their real value. The deal done, Vince decided to move on himself, and left Walford. Around the same time, Julie Cooper sold her shop and flat and moved back up North.

When Laurie Bates's on/off affair with Kathy came to an end he decided to give up his stall in Walford, an act which fuelled rumours that the Turpin Road Market was due to be closed.

Later in the year the Karims left the Square to start a new life in Bristol. This happened in the aftermath of the collapse of Ashraf's plans to arrange a marriage for Shireen, which occurred when the family of Jabbar, the prospective husband, discovered that Ashraf had a white mistress. Even as the Karims left, however, there was a glimmer of hope for the match, which both Jabbar and Shireen wanted, as the women of the two families met to discuss how the marriage might still go ahead.

In November, Mo Butcher, now in an advanced state of mental deterioration, went to live with her daughter, Joan, having become convinced that Frank meant her harm. This sad story, about the effect on a family of a parent suffering from Alzheimer's disease, had to be curtailed when actress Edna Doré decided to leave the programme. The character finally died, off-screen, at the end of 1992.

Cindy's baby, Steven, had been born on Boxing Day 1989 and in many ways his story dominated the following year, and climaxed a year after his birth, when his father Wicksy and Cindy took him away from Walford, apparently for good.

With all these characters going there was plenty of room for new ones. The middle of the year saw the threat to the market, which required new characters with market stalls for the duration of the story. This led

to the creation of Greg (Charlie Hawkins) and April (Helen Pearson) McIntosh and Jackie Stone (Richard Beale), who joined Pete in the fight to save the market.

## The Mitchells march in

Major new characters joined throughout the year, the first ones being the infamous Mitchell brothers who swept into the Square in February. The new executive producer, Michael Ferguson, wanted to introduce a couple of young men who would bring an air of danger, characters who would be unpredictable and bursting with energy. Phil (Steve McFadden) and Grant (Ross Kemp) have gone on to become major long-term characters at the heart of the series. In August their young sister Sam (Danniella Westbrook) joined them and, to the brothers' horror, became involved with Ricky Butcher.

## Enter Eddie and the Taverniers

The summer saw the introduction of a new landlord at the Vic, ex-policeman Eddie Royle (Michael Melia). Deliberately created to be a very different landlord from both Den and Frank, Eddie was designed to be an outsider so the Square and the audience would only get to know him slowly. He was joined from time to time by his father John (Paddy Joyce), who became good friends with Jules Tavernier

A new face behind the pumps at the Queen Vic as ex-copper Eddie Royle arrived in Walford with a reputation, later disproved, of having been a corrupt policeman.

(Tommy Eytle), the eldest member of the other major new addition this year. The introduction of the Taverniers, the professional couple Celestine (Leroy Golding) and Etta (Jacqui Gordon-Lawrence), and their children Clyde (Steven Woodcock), Hattie (Michelle Gayle) and Lloyd (Garey Bridges),

Three generations of the Tavernier family arrived in the summer of 1990 and moved into the house next to Dot Cotton.

heralded the first time that an entire family had joined the programme at once. It was also a well-intentioned attempt to portray a wider range of black characters than had previously been achieved.

## Other arrivals

During her time living on the streets, Diane made one fairly close friend, Disa (Jan Graveson), who appeared again at the end of the year, pregnant. On Christmas Day she left her new-born baby with Diane to be looked after.

THE FIRST 10 YEARS

Todd Carty, the only member of the original cast of *Grange Hill* to have his character (Tucker Jenkins) go on into his own series, took over the role of Mark Fowler in 1990.

The final character who should be mentioned in this section is Mark Fowler, who returned in the summer, now played by Todd Carty.

## Memorable Episodes 1990

### Episode 522 (22/2/90)

The second of a pair of episodes by Tony McHale which marked the fifth birthday of the programme, saw the christening of Steven Beale, the first appearance of Phil and Grant Mitchell, the departure of Pete's New Zealand girlfriend Barbara and Michelle's final decision not to leave Walford to live with Danny.

**Episode 532 (29/3/90)**

The second of two extraordinary episodes, also by Tony McHale, which were a radical departure from the normal *EastEnders* form. These episodes used flashbacks to tell the story of Diane's three months of living on the streets of London as a homeless person, while also telling the present story of Frank finding her and bringing her home to the Square. Powerful episodes, they returned *EastEnders* to the tradition of gritty realism that had been integral in the early episodes.

**Episode 548 (24/5/90)**

This was an unusual small-cast episode, written by P.J. Hammond, set in Dot's house and featuring Dot, Ethel, Charlie, Nick and Alistair, the bogus priest. Until this point the programme had been ambiguous as to whether Nick was a genuine born-again Christian or not—although most long-time viewers saw through him immediately—but in this episode Nick's truly evil intentions were made clear.

**Episode 560 (5/7/90)**

Written by Michael Ellis, this had three main strands, all landmarks of one kind or another. One was the first meeting between Sharon and her birth mother Carol Hanley, which ironically happened in a post-natal ward where Carol had just given birth to another child. The second was the arrival of Dot's new neighbours, the Tavernier family, and the third was the climax of the protest against the closure of the market, which ended with the destruction of Pete's stall by a bulldozer.

**Episode 598 (15/11/90)**

The second part of two special episodes, by Tony McHale (again!), these delved into Eddie's past and gave the real reason for his exit from the police force. For months there had been rumours that Eddie had been a bent copper, but in this episode the truth—that he was innocent of corruption charges—was revealed.

## Pick of the Year 1990

**Episode 580 (13/9/90)**

This was the second of two episodes that for months were known in the *EastEnders* script department as 'the Devon Cottage Climax'. Having set up the fact that Steven was Wicksy's son rather than Ian's, we knew that this was a secret that had to be blown, and the story built to this moment. With Wicksy spending some time with Cindy at her parents' house in Devon and Ian coming out of hospital, having recovered his memory of what Cindy had said to him, the stage was set. Debbie Cook's scripts took Pete and Ian, with his leg in plaster, to Devon for a confrontation that would contain elements of tragedy and farce. Particularly memorable was Ian furiously throwing bricks through the window of the house, followed by one of his crutches. This episode ended ominously with Ian finding Cindy's father's shotgun and stealing it...

Directed by Matthew Evans, these episodes not only brought the story to a good climax but also laid the roots for the next three months' worth of stories, building up to Wicksy and Cindy's final exit.

# 1991:

# That Was the Year That . . .

There were intense storylines for many of the *EastEnders* characters in 1991, with many of them experiencing unprecedented stress and heartache. The year began with some characters becoming involved in the affairs of relative strangers. Pete became concerned about the home background of little Jason, the boy who began to hang around the fruit and veg stall and help Pete out. When Pete discovered that the lad had been beaten by his own father, he had no choice but to inform the Social Services. But when he then tried to find out what had happened, he met Jason's mother who accused him of interfering in things that didn't concern him and of being a pervert! Pete was very upset that his well-intentioned actions may have left the boy worse off than before.

## Disa's story

January also saw Disa coming to the Square and living in Mo's old flat with her baby, Jasmine. After her initial rejection of the child, Disa finally began to bond with her and, with the help of Mark, Diane and Dot, she began to settle into the Square. The appearance of her step-father, Ken, complicated matters and at the end of February Ken snatched the baby. Only Dot's intervention rescued the baby for Disa, who then had to face her mother, Sandra. At the end of February Disa went home with her mother, but first they both visited Ken who was in prison on remand. Disa confronted him about his sexual abuse of both her and her sister. Sandra was forced to recognize that Disa was telling the truth, and that her baby Jasmine was conceived when Ken raped her.

## Etta faces a difficult decision

There were more baby concerns in the Tavernier family, where Etta's career as a teacher was taking off. With the opportunity to apply for a permanent position as head of her school, Etta realized that she could not afford to have any more children and decided to be sterilized. Celestine argued with her but Etta was determined to have the operation. In March she discovered that she was pregnant and, after their experience with Lloyd, who suffered from sickle cell anaemia, Etta had tests to see if the foetus had the same affected genes. It did, and in April she had the pregnancy terminated.

## Heartache for Mark

In January, Mark revealed to girlfriend Diane that he was HIV positive, and although she tried to be understanding and supportive their relationship was never quite the same again. She tried to persuade him to have counselling at the Terrance Higgins Trust and, after much reluctance, Mark agreed to go. In May Mark had to face his old girlfriend, Gill, who visited Walford. In the aftermath of her visit Mark, prompted in

> Dot Cotton, the Squares' own good Samaritan, was forever taking in waifs and strays. In 1991 it was Disa and her baby Jasmine.

part by his mum, asked Diane to marry him, but she gently turned him down and shortly afterwards left Walford to live in France. Towards the end of the year, following the example of Joe Wallace who finally came clean to his parents about being gay and being HIV positive, Mark decided to let his parents into his secret. By this time he had become involved with Rachel Kominski, who advised him against it, but Mark, tiring of pretence, went ahead and on Boxing Day told Pauline and Arthur that he was HIV positive.

## The Mitchells show their true colours

In the spring there was a story which defined exactly how dodgy the Mitchell brothers were. When a car that had been involved in a bank raid found its way to the Mitchells' garage for repair, Grant couldn't resist liberating some of the banknotes with which the boot was stuffed, not realizing that they were forgeries. After the Mitchell brothers' flat was wrecked by the raiders looking for their property (the bent printing plates and the remaining forged notes), which they were given, Grant and Phil continued to receive visits from the gang, who still wanted something. The brothers were outwitted by the villains, who recovered a number of valuable misprinted stamps that had also been in the car by getting the Mitchells to send them in the post. Perhaps the realization that he had been duped out of a good deal of money contributed to Grant's volatile mood, which exploded into violence in early April when he thought Eddie was chatting up Sharon. He beat up Eddie so savagely that he needed brain

surgery. After that, Grant tried to re-enlist in the army but was turned down after failing psychiatric tests.

Grant and Phil then became involved in a scam to use Clyde's boxing skills to make money. In the end the plan was foiled, partly because Eddie tipped off the police. This gave Grant a possible motive when Eddie was found murdered in the Square.

Over the summer Grant had patched up his relationship with Sharon, and plans were being made for a wedding until Grant was arrested. After his release, Sharon learned the truth about his frequent nightmares and blackouts, which dated back to his time on active service in the Falklands War. There he had killed an enemy soldier, no more than a boy really, who was unarmed, and Grant had never been able to come to terms with his death. After this the couple became much closer and on Boxing Day they were married.

## Eddie's murder

In many ways the murder of Eddie Royle was the nexus for most of the storylines during 1991, with many separate stories leading into the murder, and then a number of new strands emerging from the aftermath. One of the stories which was a most important feed for Eddie's murder did not seem to have any connection at first.

This was the story of Nick's latest reappearance in Walford, this time as a complete heroin addict. At first Dot was ruthless in her determination to have nothing to do with her son but, after the death of Charlie, Dot

> Poor Eddie Royle needed brain surgery after a jealous Grant Mitchell beat him up.

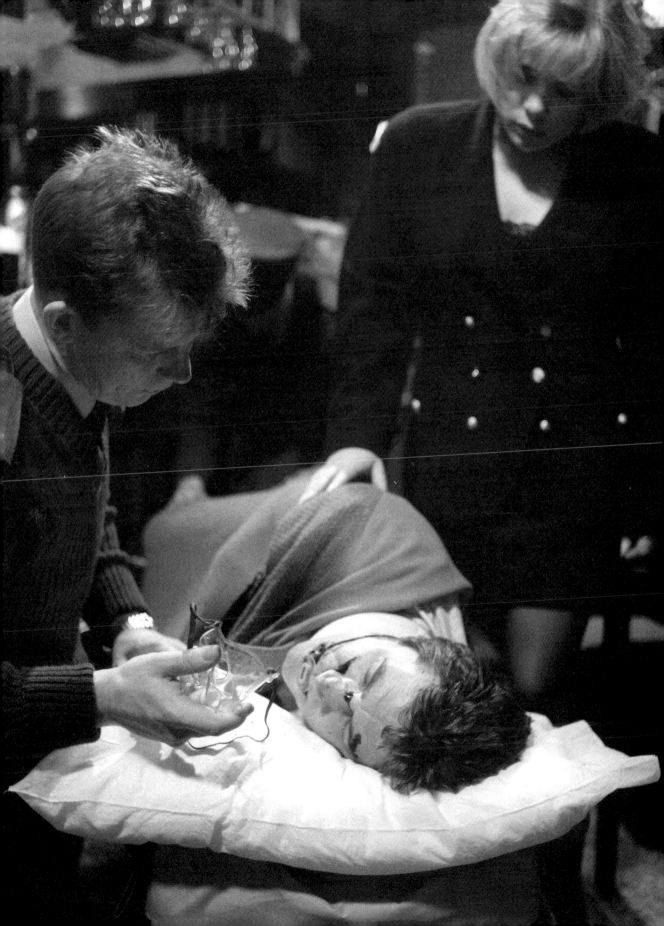

The Meal Machine — but Ian's interest was more in making money than food. Helped by his assistant Hattie, Ian's business went from strength to strength.

changed her mind and took Nick in. She was determined to break Nick's habit and embarked on a programme of cutting down his heroin intake day by day. Nick agreed to the idea but secretly stole and cheated money to supplement the cash that Dot was getting for him. Nick even advertised the house as being available for rent and pocketed the deposits of people who wanted to live there. When it became clear that Nick had failed to keep to the programme Dot decided to get tough and locked Nick in his bedroom, and arranged with Pete to have the room's windows boarded up. Nick was forced to break his habit the hard way— cold turkey—and his resulting paranoia and craving for heroin led him to escape from the room for a fateful meeting with Eddie Royle.

### Ian gets harder than ever

Ian Beale, entrepreneur, went from strength to strength. In January he had problems with his waitresses and Sharon stopped working for him because of his exploitative working practices. Ian quickly bounced back and continued his catering business, using Hattie Tavernier as a waitress. In March Ian investigated taking on the lease of the Dagmar. He planted one of the computers that were stolen from the council by Grant and Phil in the pub so that Jackie Stone, who was squatting on the site, would be evicted. Having succeeded, much to his father's horror, Ian then tried to sell the café to his mother. In the end Kathy, Pauline and Frank teamed up to make the purchase, and prevented Ian getting a widely inflated price for it.

### Michelle leaves home again

Feeling herself in a rut, Michelle started to think about a new job and home. When Rachel Kominski arrived in March and advertised for a lodger Michelle thought she might get the room, but when Rachel found out that Vicki would come too she let the room to a girl called Karen instead. Michelle got herself a new job, selling time-share holiday apartments, through a business associate of Ian's. The problem was it carried no wage— commission was paid only if a certain quota of sales was reached. In May, Rachel, having heard of the injustice, intervened and embarrassed the company into paying Michelle what she was owed. Karen then decided to leave Walford and Michelle moved in with Rachel.

EastEnders
THE FIRST 10 YEARS

For a while things were difficult for Michelle—Rachel was so different, with her education and her middle-class background and friends—but they became firm friends and in the summer Rachel persuaded her lodger that she should go back into education. Encouraged by Rachel, Michelle began studying for a diploma later in the year at the local Polytechnic (which later became a University). Another result of her new living arrangements was that Michelle finally got together with Clyde Tavernier. They had been friends for a while, united as single parents, and when some people began to speculate that Michelle and Rachel were gay, Michelle found herself sleeping with Clyde.

Later in the year when Clyde was hiding from the police, after being accused of killing Eddie, he tried to collect his son Kofi and ended up hiding out in Rachel's house.

Murder in the Square. But whodunnit? Clyde Tavernier, Grant Mitchell or nasty Nick Cotton? But Nick was locked in his room at his mum's, wasn't he …?

## Goodbye, Eddie

The big story of the year, of course, was the murder of Eddie Royle. He kept managing to rub people up the wrong way. The very fact that he was an ex-policeman made a number of his customers nervous and he seemed to fare no better in his personal life. His on/off relationship with Kathy was complicated still further when his father reintroduced him to his old flame, Eibhlin O'Donnell. He made Sharon choose between her job at the Vic and her relationship with Grant—when Sharon chose Grant, Eddie sacked her. She then took him to an industrial tribunal, for unfair dismissal, and won her case but Eddie still refused to give her her job back. Sharon told Grant that she would marry him, but only if he got her the tenancy of The Queen Vic. Meanwhile Eddie was further alienating the community by trying to change the name of the pub. By the time he was killed, a number of people had good reason not to be too upset.

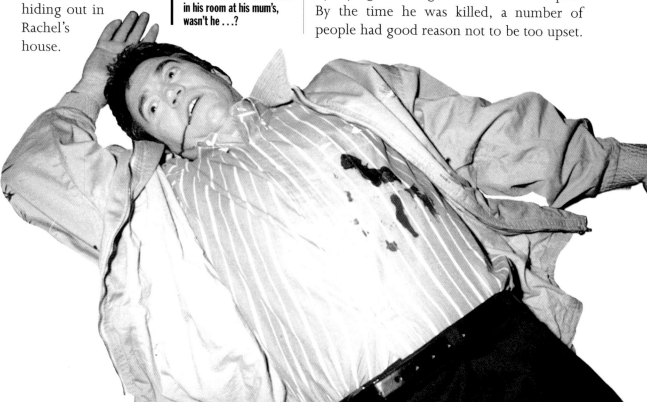

## Comings 'n' Goings 1991

After a few years of hectic comings and goings of regulars, 1991 saw a slight decrease in the speed of these arrivals and departures. Most of the new characters who appeared during the year were temporary, seen only for the duration of their story. In some ways the more significant movements occurred behind the scenes, because executive producer Michael Ferguson decided to move on towards the end of the year. At the same time both his producers, Corinne Hollingsworth and Pat Sandys, also decided to leave, so by the end of the year there was a complete change in the people responsible for making the programme.

### New faces in Albert Square

On-screen there were only two new regulars who appeared during 1991. The first of these was Rachel Kominski, the latest in a long line of middle-class characters who have appeared in the programme. Played by Jacquetta May with a good deal of warmth and humour, she managed to transcend the slightly clichéd, middle-class college lecturer that she could easily have been. With her close involvement with both Mark and Michelle Fowler, Rachel managed to integrate into the life of the Square slightly better than some of the other middle-class characters in the programme's history.

In October the second regular of the year to join was Steve Elliot (Mark Monero), the young black cook with ambitions to see the world. First seen working as a chef in the Pizza Parlour, which by now had opened up in the premises once occupied by Den's

Steve Elliot, a man with big dreams, and Hattie who thought he was the man to make *her* dreams come true.

Strokes wine bar, Steve was quickly offered a job at Ian Beale's Meal Machine. Steve initially turned the job down but Ian, recognizing his talent, was determined to get his man, and used Hattie's friendship with him to change his mind.

Although many of the other characters who appeared during this year were temporary they were not without their significance. Eibhlin O'Donnell (Mary Conlon), an old flame of Eddie Royle's, was brought over by his father John from Ireland, in the hope of resurrecting their stalled relationship. Unfortunately Eddie had become interested in Kathy and John's timing couldn't have been worse, but within a few months Eddie had changed his mind again and had proposed to Eibhlin.

Karen (Adjoa Andoh), first seen as a singer at the Vic one night, was Rachel's original lodger when she moved into the Karims' old house. She was briefly involved with Clyde, before moving on to pursue her singing career in pastures new. Later in the year, now living in Portsmouth, Karen was able to give refuge to Clyde and Michelle when they were on the run from the police.

One of the stories that dominated 1991 was Mark's coming to terms with his HIV positive status, and a number of new characters were needed specifically for that storyline. The first of these was Lorna (Cathy Murphy), a girl Mark met in a disco after rowing with his then girlfriend Diane. Realizing that a 'normal' relationship was impossible for him, Mark quickly ended their affair, which had hardly begun. Mark then had to deal with the reappearance in his life of Gill (Susanna Dawson), the girl he had lived with when he had been in Newcastle. At first he denied that he was HIV positive, but later told her the truth.

The next visiting character was Joe Wallace (Jason Rush), another cook, who found work at the Meal Machine. Joe was both gay and HIV positive, and he recognized Mark from HIV/Aids counselling sessions. When Ian learned that Joe was gay he surprised everyone by not giving a damn. However, when Ian then found that Joe was HIV positive he immediately fired him. Joe left the Square on the same night as Eddie's murder and was later a vital witness. When Clyde was arrested and charged with Eddie's murder, it was Joe's evidence that secured his release and forced Nick Cotton into a confession.

## Departures

On the debit side in this year there was the off-screen death of sad old Charlie Cotton, killed in a crash while driving a lorry. Diane Butcher decided to abandon her art college course and begin a new life in France, much to Frank's horror, and Disa and her new baby went home to Sunderland with her mother Sandra. The final exit of the year happened in September with the brutal and unexpected murder of Eddie Royle, in the middle of the Square, which shocked everyone and paved the way for Sharon to become Queen of The Vic. In the short term the storyline produced material for many characters over the following months, but in the long term the one who gained most was Sharon. Eddie's death paved the way for her to become landlady of The Queen Vic.

## Memorable Episodes 1991

### Episode 614 (10/1/91)

Written by Tony McHale, this was an important episode in which Mark's secret was finally revealed to the audience, when Diane found out that he was HIV positive.

### Episode 664 (4/7/91)

Written by Debbie Cook, this was the second of two episodes which followed Ricky and Sam's attempt to elope to Gretna Green. With Frank, Pat, Grant, Phil, Peggy Mitchell and her boyfriend Kevin all in hot pursuit, these episodes were essentially a farcical chase, climaxing in the register office wedding of the kids, with Frank and Pat in attendance. As ever, despite the Scottish setting, the recording of these episodes was achieved rather closer to home, with parts of Hertfordshire becoming Scotland.

Married at last – Sam and Ricky finally made it to the register office after a farce-like chase round the country.

### Episode 666 (11/7/91)

This episode, written by Linda Dearsley and Steve Waye, was dominated by Dot's reaction to the news that Charlie had died, and her trip to identify the body. Actress June Brown was very upset that her screen husband was being written out in this manner and begged the producers to change their minds. It was felt, however, that only a shock this great would persuade Dot to give Nick another chance after his attempt to kill her in the previous year.

Back in Walford and in a bad way – Nick Cotton, now a heroin addict and needing his mum!

## Episode 680 (29/8/91)

This intense episode featured the beginnings of Dot's 'tough love' treatment of her son's heroin addiction, as Pete boarded up the windows and helped Dot to lock Nick in his room all day. Meanwhile Sharon was winning her claim for unfair dismissal from the pub. The episode was written by story-line editor Andrew Holden.

## Episode 683 (10/9/91)

This was the big autumn launch episode for 1991, and climaxed with the unexpected murder of unfortunate Eddie Royle. Written by Tony McHale, it finished with the dramatic, if slightly misleading, cliffhanger featuring Clyde in the gardens standing over Eddie's body and holding a knife. Originally the plan had been for the audience to know from the outset that Nick was responsible but this was changed to exploit the whodunnit angle.

On the quayside Clyde and Michelle consider a future together in France ...

## Pick of the Year 1991

### Episode 702 (14/11/91)

The second of a pair of episodes written by Tony Jordan as the second double-bank of the year, these came as the climax of the mini-storyline of Clyde on the run and had Michelle, Vicki, Clyde and Kofi attempting to get to France to begin a new life. Played as if it really could be the last appearance of Michelle, who had been so central to the programme, there was a strong sense of tension as the episode built to the inevitable ending, with Michelle and Clyde arrested by the police on the verge of boarding a private boat that would have taken them to France.

Directed by Mike Dormer, this is one of the most exciting thriller episodes of *EastEnders*. It also allowed a new side of both Clyde and Michelle to be seen, and put real pressure on their already fragile relationship.

# That Was the Year That . . .

Towards the end of 1991 there was a flurry of activity behind the scenes at EastEnders, when Leonard Lewis and Helen Greaves joined the programme as co-producers. Together they formulated a new regime in which the writers of the programme would 'drive' the series. Individual stories would be written and agreed or discarded at regular story conferences, and the progression of those stories would be the responsibility of the individual episode writers, with the script department providing guidance rather than prescriptive episodic storylines. With stories growing and developing in this new organic way, the writers were freed to write what they wanted—and the script editor's job of keeping the programme's continuity and tone intact became even harder!

The stories during 1992, while this new system evolved, were complex and lively. A danger of the new way of working was that stories wouldn't evolve slowly, as they had in the past, and that events would occur suddenly and without warning. In practice, however, the stories were inter-related and fed each other remarkably well.

### The Butchers' bad time

It was a year of great changes for the Butchers, beginning with a huge tax demand and swiftly followed by a large VAT bill.

Taking the advice of his accountant, Frank decided to sell his beloved Mercedes and found a willing punter in the form of a friend of Grant's, one Nigel Bates. Grant tried to intervene as a middle-man and make a profit on the deal for himself, but Frank out-manoeuvred him. Despite his success with the Merc, Frank was still desperately in need of money and in April he sold the Bed and Breakfast. Unfortunately the buyer was only interested in both the Bed and Breakfast *and* the adjoining house, in which the Butchers were living. Pat, more than slightly annoyed at being made homeless, took herself off to a hotel. Luckily Frank was able to secure the downstairs flat next to the Fowlers.

In the summer, things looked up for Frank when he was able to give Phil an alibi when Phil took his brother's place in a raid on a bookie's. Frank demanded his Merc back as the price of his silence and Grant had to buy the car back from a distressed Nigel.

The latter half of the year saw Pat deciding to start a business of her own and forming PatCabs, a minicab service operating out of Frank's Portakabin. For a while things went well, with PatCabs doing better than the car lot itself, but on Christmas Eve tragedy struck the Butchers. Pat, while doing a short run for a regular customer when one of her drivers was ill, had an accident in which she hit a teenage girl. When breathalysed she was found to be just over the limit. On New Year's Eve, against advice, Pat tried to find out how the girl was, and was devastated to learn that she had died. Meanwhile Frank was coping with his own sad news, as his sister told him of Mo's death.

## Mr and Mrs Mitchell

Another story which twisted and turned throughout the year was that of the new owners of The Queen Vic—Grant and Sharon Mitchell. The newly-weds soon woke up to the reality of marriage, with Grant wanting to start a family while Sharon preferred to concentrate on making the Vic a success first. In the spring Phil began an affair with the mysterious Anne, and surprised his brother and sister-in-law by bringing her back to the Vic for the night.

Feeling hemmed in by his marriage, Grant began to long for his old life and in June he got involved in a planned raid on a betting shop. When Sharon became suspicious of his activities and threatened to end their relationship for good, Grant got Phil to take his place as getaway driver. The raiders, Steer and Keating, were incompetent bunglers, and one shot the other in the foot by mistake. When Phil stopped to help the injured Keating, Steer drove off and left them. Phil managed to get away but the

A rose between two thorns? The question troubling Sharon was a simple one — did she marry the wrong brother?

police were very suspicious, and only Frank and Pete's false alibis saved Phil from arrest.

In July, Grant and Sharon began to argue over money, and after a birthday party for Michelle, which Sharon paid for and at which Grant behaved badly, they had a major row. During the row Sharon confessed that she had carried on taking the Pill because she didn't want a baby with Grant. He went berserk and smashed up the pub. After that, Grant disappeared for a few weeks, leaving Phil to comfort Sharon in her hour of need. For a while, Sharon wondered if she had married the wrong brother. When Grant returned, he and Sharon made a fragile peace—she apologized for deceiving him, he apologized for his anger. Despite his promises to try harder he immediately returned to his old ways, choosing to be out with his mates rather than be there for Sharon, and leaving Phil to help out at the Vic in his place. Oblivious of the growing attraction between his wife and his brother, Grant had another argument with Sharon at the beginning of September and went out for the night with his mate Nigel. At the end of the evening the inevitable release of pent-up desire led to Phil and Sharon going to bed together, but when Grant returned Sharon chose him rather than Phil, thus priming a bomb with a long fuse. It would be another two years before it exploded.

High drama continued to focus on the Vic, however, as Grant found himself in further trouble with local villains. Having learned his lesson over the bookie raid, he had turned down the offer from some heavies to be the driver for a wages snatch but had given them the name of a mate who could do the job. When the driver disappeared with all the money, the villains blamed Grant and demanded—with menaces—that he make good their loss. At first Grant was unimpressed but Jason, who was the nutter making the threats, had a reputation for being totally psycho and when he turned up in the Vic and intimidated Sharon, Grant knew that he had to act. When the Community Centre burned down, after an arson attack by some local kids, Grant thought he would do the same to the Vic and claim the insurance. Phil told him what a poor idea this was but Grant was desperate and went ahead, not realizing that the pub wasn't empty as he had thought but that Sharon and Roly were in there. Luckily, they were rescued in time. The insurance money paid for the refurbishment of the Vic, but was not enough to cover the money owed to Jason. While Grant took Sharon for a week's holiday in Brighton to recuperate, Phil tracked down the missing driver and recovered the money.

In November, Michelle and Sharon had a girls' night out at a gig at Michelle's college, but it turned to disaster when their other halves, Clyde and Grant arrived looking for them. Grant was convinced that Sharon was seeing another man but it was Michelle they discovered in bed with a student called Jack. When Grant found Sharon they had a terrific row, during which Grant confessed that he had set fire to the pub. Sharon told them that they were finished and walked off with Michelle. After that, things went from bad

to worse in the Vic, with Grant deciding to give it all up and put the pub on the market.

At Christmas, Phil persuaded Grant to go away for a while to let things cool down. With Grant away, Sharon and Phil would have had Christmas alone together in the pub but for the presence of Ricky and Sam, who had been evicted from squatting in Mo's flat and were also living at the Vic.

## Arthur reveals his sexy side

The other big story of 1992 was known as 'The Bonk of the Year' and was one of the most outrageous ideas ever to be pitched at a story conference. Tony McHale wondered what would happen if Arthur Fowler had an affair. At first most of the people at the conference laughed, thinking it was a joke, but Tony was serious.

Like all good stories it built up slowly. The year had begun in turmoil for the Fowlers, with Arthur refusing to come to terms with the fact that Mark was HIV positive. After a difficult period, in which Arthur and Pauline actually came to blows over the subject, Arthur finally came round after seeing a father treating his son badly in a pub. At the same time, Pauline persuaded Mark to start working with Arthur again in his gardening business. Over the next few days, while working on the garden of a lonely woman called Mrs Hewitt, the atmosphere between father and son began to thaw. Finally, in March, Mark decided to stop working with his dad, because they kept rubbing each other up the wrong way. For the first time in ages they were then able to hug each other, realizing they needed

a little distance between them in order to be close. Without Mark to help him, Arthur needed an assistant and advertised to try and fill the post. He was surprised when Mrs Hewitt turned up in Walford, enquiring about the job. She wanted it for her son Jonathan, but when he proved lazy and unreliable an embarrassed Mrs Hewitt took his place as Arthur's gardening assistant.

> Seeds of future stories were planted when Arthur demonstrated his green fingers to lonely Christine Hewitt.

At the end of May, a phone call from New Zealand brought news that Kenny Beale had been in a car crash and, with Pete's financial help, Pauline decided to go and visit him. (In fact, Pauline had to be written out to allow Wendy Richard time to make a series of *Grace and Favour*.) While Pauline was away, Christine Hewitt became a regular visitor to Albert Square, causing a certain amount of gossip, and it was clear that she was becoming very fond of Arthur. For a

while Pete tried to remind her that Arthur was a married man—and married to his sister, to boot—but then he found himself taking her out! In August it all came to a head, when Christine actually made a pass at Arthur. He turned her down and she disappeared, sending him a letter and a photo telling him how she felt. Arthur knew that he had to face her one last time, and visited her in her house. There he told her that he felt something for her too, but he was married and he loved his wife. They said goodbye and the matter seemed over.

When Pauline came home, however, she learned all about it from gossips like Dot. Although she believed Arthur when he explained what had happened, all that changed when she found Christine's letter and photo. Pauline went to see Mrs Hewitt to discover the truth, and found Christine to be a sad, lonely figure who drank too much in the afternoons. Pauline was persuaded to forgive Arthur and start over but then Arthur, worried that Pauline might contact her, went to see Mrs Hewitt himself.

Over the next few weeks Arthur kept finding excuses to drop in on Christine, until she told him not to come again unless he meant business. On Christmas Eve Arthur sneaked away to be with Mrs Hewitt and they ended up in bed!

### The return of Willmott-Brown

Other major stories were threaded through the year. Willmott-Brown appeared again at the start of 1992, buying the flats from the Mitchell brothers and moving into his old house before being confronted by Kathy and Pete and persuaded to leave Walford for good. Kathy then went away for five months, to stay with her brother and to recover from the trauma of seeing Willmott-Brown again. (In reality, actress Gillian Taylforth was on maternity leave, and gave birth to her daughter Jessica in January 1992.) When Kathy returned, she found that Pauline had gone off, without notice, to New Zealand and when she returned Kathy bought her share of the café.

### Ian's vulnerability emerges

Ian began the year by giving Hattie new responsibilities at the Meal Machine to entice her back to work for him. Steve, disappointed by Hattie's decision to rejoin Ian's business, left Walford but returned in April, determined to make his own success. While he was out of the picture Ian made a pass at Hattie, but a swift knee in his groin told him that she wanted their relationship to be platonic. Ian's loneliness was revealed when he invited a client to dinner and made out that he had a partner. When Hattie refused to play his girlfriend for the night Ian hired a girl from an escort agency for the role. He then tried to get a date with the woman, who refused, and Ian took to kerb-crawling round Kings Cross to pick up prostitutes.

When Kathy returned in the summer, Ian confessed how lonely he was and how much he missed Cindy and Steven. An affair with an older woman, who he met when she employed him, didn't last long and then the Meal Machine was rocked by an infestation of cockroaches. The only way to raise the money to have the place fumigated was to

cash in some old insurance policies that he had taken out with Cindy. Needing her signature, he tracked her down and discovered that she was living in a tiny bedsit, having been abandoned by Wicksy some months before. Carefully, Ian began wooing Cindy again, showing that he had grown up since she had left him. He persuaded her to come and spend Christmas with him in Walford, in secret, and he was delighted when she agreed. In fact, Ian and Cindy's happy Christmas was in contrast to the general tragedy, death and misery elsewhere in the Square!

## Comings 'n' Goings 1992

A number of new regular characters made their debuts during 1992, and for the most part they appeared gradually, making an initial appearance and then joining the programme full-time a couple of months later. This allowed the producers and writers to create new characters and see them brought to life by actors before committing them to a long contract.

## The arrival of Tricky Dicky

The major exception to this was the creation of Tricky Dicky, the new man-we-love-to-hate. Richard Cole was designed to be a bit of a lad, a charming womanizer, and was supposed to be a Cockney according to his biography, written by Tony Jordan. However, when the producers saw Ian Reddington read for the part they knew that they had found Tricky Dicky, and the character's background was changed. Richard Cole was the market inspector and

Second time lucky? Ian tracked down his errant wife, Cindy, and began to woo her anew at the end of 1992, spending a happy Christmas together.

was involved in sec-
uring a pitch for
Rachel, who decided
to take a stall after her

*An unlikely romance developed from would be market trader Rachel Kominski's run-in with 'Tricky Dicky' Cole.*

job at the Poly was cut. Unable to resist a
challenge, Richard pursued her but as soon
as he had bedded her he moved on to
new prey—Kathy. When he won a holiday
through the raffle at the Traders' Christmas
Ball—to cries of 'fix', of course—he invited
Kathy to go with him. Possibly to spite Pete,
who was horrified at the idea, she said yes,
and Tricky Dicky made another conquest.

## Other newcomers

The other new characters made more ten-
tative first appearances. Christine Hewitt
(Lizzie Power) first appeared in February as
the latest employer of Arthur's gardening
skills, but in the summer she returned to
work with him. Mandy Salter (Nicola
Stapleton) visited the Butchers in March,
when her mother Lorraine (Linda Henry)
was in hospital. She left thinking that she
was unwanted, and then returned in July to
live in Walford. Nigel Bates (Paul Bradley)
also appeared in March, when he bought

Frank's Mercedes. When his mother died later in the year Nigel returned to Walford and became Dot's lodger. In November, a visit to Michelle's college introduced a number of her fellow students. Two of them, Shelley (Nicole Arumugam) and Jack (James Gilbey), would appear more regularly the following year.

## Brief visitors

The year began with yet another visit from Willmott-Brown, now released after serving his sentence for rape but still obsessed with Kathy. Phil had a short-term girlfriend Anne (Cassie Stuart), who turned out to be a habitual liar. Mrs Hewitt's spaced-out, New Age son Jonathan (Jonny Lee Miller) helped Arthur for a while in the spring. Ian's work brought him into contact with Mike and Marilyn Monroe (John Salthouse and Sadie Shimmin) and later in the year with Ronnie Bains (Lesley Nightingale). Grant ran into trouble with amateur villains Steer and Keating and then, in the autumn, got embroiled with Jason, who was much more dangerous. In December Dot met Donald (Robert Wilson), a blind pianist, who helped organize her carol concert, and Sam met a man called Clive (Sean Gallagher) who gave her a glimpse of the lifestyle she aspired to.

The year also saw the welcome return of Cindy, as Ian tried to correct his past mistakes and the programme-makers tried to bring back to the series a useful and popular character.

## A few farewells

There weren't just arrivals in the Square. The summer saw the departure of half of the Tavernier family, when Celestine got a new job, a significant promotion, in Nor-

Perhaps *EastEnders'* most poignant wedding to date. Mark and Gill tied the knot mere hours before the bride died from AIDS.

wich. Etta was unwilling to move but after Lloyd got himself into trouble with the police by joy-riding, she decided that a fresh start for the family might be the best idea. She continued to commute to her school in Walford until the end of term, then joined Celestine and Lloyd in Norwich.

We also saw the death of an original EastEnder when Ethel's faithful dog Willy succumbed to old age and had to be put down. Sadly not long after his last appearance as Willy, the dog who played him also passed away.

June saw another death—this time it was Gill, who married Mark only the day before she died. Carefully researched, Gill's death was the inevitable conclusion to the Aids storyline and was handled with great care. Despite this, some viewers were upset at the naming of the exact disease that Gill was suffering from at the time of her death, as it is frequently unconnected with Aids. For actress Susanna Dawson, the experience of playing a person living with, and dying from, Aids was so intense that she co-produced an educational video based on the subject for use in schools and wrote a book, *The Gill and Mark Story*, to accompany it.

## Memorable Episodes 1992

### Episode 728 (13/2/92)
Another small-cast episode of *EastEnders*, this was a three-hander with Pete, Kathy and James Willmott-Brown. Written by Debbie Cook, this episode allowed Kathy finally to lay to rest the ghost of her rape and convince Pete that their marriage was well and truly over. It also gave Gillian Taylforth a terrific acting challenge, just before she went on maternity leave.

### Episode 747 (21/4/92)
This was a typical Tony Jordan episode, dominated by the Miss Queen Vic competition, which the Mitchell brothers nearly fixed. In the end the honest winner was Sam, Ricky's wife.

### Episode 766 (25/6/92)
Written by Debbie Cook, this was the second episode of the first double-bank of the year, and was directed by Leonard Lewis. In the

first episode of the week, Mark and Gill had been married, and this episode opened with them enjoying their honeymoon in a hotel. Gill began to feel ill again and had to return to the hospice. There, later that day, she died. Although in many ways the episode was sad and downbeat it was not without its positive aspects, as Mark talked to his sister about his own mortality.

## Episode 800 (22/10/92)

This episode, written by Tony Jordan, celebrated Sharon's birthday with Grant's act of arson at The Queen Vic. What Grant didn't know, as he set fire to the place, was that Sharon had returned from her party at Michelle's and was upstairs. This was also the episode in which Ian finally got to speak to Cindy again.

A special effects extravaganza on the Elstree Lot as The Queen Vic burns. It must have been a nervous night for the *EastEnders* producers — one false move and the whole of Albert Square could have been ablaze.

### Episode 805 (10/11/92)

This was notable for being the first of a pair written and directed by Tony McHale. A double-bank, these episodes followed Michelle and Sharon to a gig at Michelle's college and the fun that ensued when Clyde and Grant came looking for them. This was probably the first time Michelle's 'other life' as a student became credible in the series, and a good example of the way a location can enhance the lot material to give a sense of the real world that the characters live in.

### Pick of the Year 1992

### Episode 786 (3/9/92)

For personal reasons, my most memorable episode of 1992 was the last one, Episode 820, which went out on New Year's Eve. That's because it was the first episode that I wrote for the series, but I wouldn't be so immodest as to choose that for my Pick of the Year!

Instead, I have chosen Episode 786, which

was the second three-hander of 1992, this time featuring Phil, Grant and Sharon. This

> Michelle and Sharon's girls' night out was a great success until their other halves, Clyde and Grant, turned up!

was the second of two episodes written by Tony Jordan, in which the sexual chemistry between Phil and his sister-in-law, Sharon, finally erupted in passion. In the second episode, which happened immediately after Phil had slept with Sharon for the first time, the protagonists had to deal with the aftermath and the possibility that Grant would discover what had happened.

Phil made it quite clear to Sharon that he was prepared to risk everything and tell Grant, but when the crunch came Sharon decided to choose Grant rather than Phil.

Sue Dunderdale was the director, and the performances from Letitia Dean, Ross Kemp and Steve McFadden made for a memorable half-hour of high-tension drama. In a year full of very powerful episodes, this still had to be the pick of the bunch.

## 1993:

# That Was the Year That . . .

By the end of 1992, Helen Greaves had decided to move on and Leonard Lewis became executive producer, joined initially by Barbara Emile (one of his team of script editors) and later by Diana Kyle as producers. Veteran writer Tony McHale also joined the team as story consultant to assist in the plotting of the programme.

### A bad start for Michelle

Albert Square was busy in 1993, with over forty individual stories featured over the twelve months. Early in the year Michelle began to receive unwanted attention from Jack Woodman, the student she had had a one-night stand with the previous November. He started to turn up in Albert Square, with various excuses, and then began to get additional coaching for his college work from Michelle's landlady, Rachel. Despite enlisting Phil's assistance in an attempt to scare the lad off, in the end Michelle had to contact Jack's parents and confront them with his irrational behaviour.

March saw further trauma for Michelle when Vicki was kidnapped, immediately after Rachel moved away from Walford. Luckily the woman who took Vicki made a fundamental mistake when buying some

In 1993 Michelle faced every mother's nightmare when Vicki was kidnapped. Thankfully this story had a happy ending.

presents for the child, and the police were able to trace and rescue Michelle's daughter.

## The Butchers hit more tough times

The year began badly for Pat and Frank as well. In January Pat had to begin to cope with the guilt of having killed the girl on Christmas Eve. The situation was made worse when the girl's mother confronted Pat after her appearance in the Magistrates' Court, at which the case was referred to the Crown Court. By May, Pat had started the healing process and Frank began to see a brighter future. However, when she appeared in court Pat was given a prison sentence.

The summer months were hard for Frank and Ricky, who tried to carry on as normal and, in the autumn when Pat returned, the family struggled to make a new start. Realizing that the flat at number 43 was too small for them all, Frank arranged to buy the house next door, number 41, and the Butcher family was completed when Janine came home, having spent most of the year with her big sister Claire. The resurrected cab company, now called F and P Cabs, was struggling to survive and, when faced with the vicious dirty tactics of a rival cab firm, Frank was forced to admit defeat and give it up. With only the car lot left from their once great business empire—and even that suffering in the recession—the Butchers ended the year with severe financial problems.

## Sadness for the Beales

It was a year of ups and downs for the Beale family, too. After her Christmas and New Year visit, Cindy left Walford again, only to return within weeks having lost her flat. Ian was only too happy to take her and Steven in, but when Kathy heard about this, she paid Cindy a visit and told her to leave, which she did. Eventually Ian found out that this was the only reason that Cindy had gone and he set about finding her again. This time he brought her home to Walford for good. Things did not run smoothly, however, and Cindy proved to be very jealous of Hattie's role at the Meal Machine. Cindy also reverted to her old ways and became the focus for Tricky Dicky's amorous intentions for a while. In August, she announced that she was pregnant, news that Ian was delighted with until the rumours that Tricky Dicky was the father began to spread. For a few awkward months it appeared that Ian would be heartbroken again, but Cindy maintained her innocence and eventually Ian accepted it. In December Cindy gave birth, prematurely, to twins, and called them Pete and Lucy.

On the business front, Ian found it impossible to keep the Meal Machine going from his home and, towards the end of the year, he had to accept a job at the café from his mum, in order to provide for his newly enlarged family.

At the beginning of the year a chance meeting seemed to offer the hope of happiness at last for hapless Pete Beale, when he met Rose, an old friend of Pauline's from their school-days. A romance began which was curtailed when it became clear that not

**Pete Beale hoped to make it third time lucky with Rose, having failed in two marriages, but the writers had other ideas...**

only was Rose married, but she was married to a local gangster, Alfie Chapman, who had an awesome reputation for violence. Although Alfie was safely locked up in prison, his family were not and they made it quite clear that they did not approve of Rose seeing Pete. In March, Rose learned that Alfie had a terminal disease and she decided to stop seeing Pete to nurse Alfie through his remaining months. Sadly, this was not to be, and in May she re-entered Pete's life, telling him that she missed him. Pete and Rose then went into hiding, knowing that they could only enjoy a life together somewhere away from the Chapmans. In December, when Alfie died, Pete planned to return to Walford but he and Rose died in a car accident, an 'accident' almost certainly arranged by the Chapmans.

### Difficulties for the Fowlers

For the Fowler household, the year was dominated by the secret affair of Arthur and Christine Hewitt, which had started at Christmas 1992. Despite Christine's encouragement, Arthur never really felt at ease with having to lie to Pauline, but things became easier when Pauline herself became the subject of another man's attention. Danny Taurus was the stage name of an East End rock and roller who had nearly been famous locally when Pete and Pauline were teenagers. Now a rather pathetic pub singer who dreamed of making a comeback and storming the charts, Danny was stunned to meet a girl he had always fancied when they were at school together. Danny and Pauline went on a few platonic dates—Pauline's

motive being to see if Arthur might respond to a bit of competition—and then Danny asked Pauline to go away with him. Pauline turned him down and Danny went off, still hoping for his big break.

Meanwhile, Kathy's decision to open the café in the evenings as a bistro gave Mrs Hewitt an opportunity to see more of Arthur—she applied to be Kathy's bistro cook. Not realizing that the affair was going on, Kathy gave her the job. Working in Walford was not enough for Christine, however, and she began to make greater demands on Arthur, asking him to choose between her and Pauline and to live with her. In September, under pressure from Mrs Hewitt, Arthur finally told Pauline the truth, and tried to tell her that he wanted her, not Christine. Hurt, embarrassed and angry, Pauline refused to listen to him and threw him out. For a while he stayed at Mark's flat and then left the Square altogether, finally returning when Michelle tracked him down to the hostel he was staying in. Only when Pete died did Pauline begin to warm to Arthur again, as he helped her cope with the funeral arrangements for her beloved twin brother.

### Tangled love at the Vic

At the Vic it was a year of struggle, beginning with Phil failing to persuade Grant to give up the idea of selling the pub. Angry with both brothers, Sharon walked out to visit Angie—a visit made necessary by actress Letitia Dean's appearances in pantomime at the end of 1992. When Sharon returned, in March, to find the mess that the brothers were making of running the

pub, she took over. In the row that followed, Grant hit her. Michelle, protective of her friend as always, called the police but when they arrived Grant lost his temper and began attacking them. One of the policemen he hit was badly injured, so the police were able to oppose bail and Grant found himself in prison on remand. While he was gone, Sharon and Phil lived as man and wife at the Vic for a while, experiencing what might have been if she had chosen him

Walford's answer to Elvis, the legendary Danny Taurus, took a shine to Pauline in 1993.

**Another happy Walford wedding? Not exactly – Phil would later discover that this was a marriage of *in*convenience.**

for good—he even asked Sharon's permission before he took another woman back to the Vic for a meal. Sharon was surprised to find that the woman was not an airheaded bimbo and that Grant didn't end the evening in bed with her. When Sharon asked Grant about this, he explained that he was still in love with her. By the end of June, Sharon and Grant were back together.

On the rebound, Phil found himself in a marriage of convenience to Nadia, a Romanian refugee. When Steve left Hattie days before their wedding, Phil offered Hattie a lift to Portsmouth, where she hoped to catch up with Steve before he could board the ship he was sailing on. Hattie then decided not to tell Steve that she was pregnant, and they parted. Meanwhile, Phil met Nadia in a Portsmouth bar and, feeling sorry for her, agreed to marry her so she could remain in the country, with her boyfriend Marco.

In the autumn Phil finally began a romance with Kathy, a liaison that had first been suggested by the script department three years before but had been rejected in favour of Kathy getting involved with Eddie Royle. Inevitably, Nadia returned to Walford in November, needing Phil to play her husband in more realistic ways to prevent her being deported. Jealous of her husband's 'real' girlfriend, Nadia made things as difficult as possible for Kathy and Phil, and finally seduced Phil at Christmas and slept with him. Phil didn't help his problems by failing to tell Kathy the truth about Nadia in the first place.

in the first place. Neither of the lovers was prepared to tell Grant the truth, however, and when Grant came out of prison a changed man, Sharon realized that she and Phil would never be an item.

For a while, Grant continued to live at the Vic and work there, but not as Sharon's husband. Grant appeared to have changed

## The trials and tribulations of Aidan and Mandy

Another major story which ran throughout 1993 was that of the young lovers Aidan and Mandy. Aidan first appeared in January, an apprentice at Arthur's beloved Walford Town football club who was having problems with his digs. Arthur arranged for Aidan to lodge with the Fowlers instead, and then he had to help the shy lad from Ireland cope with life in the capital. In the company of Ricky and Mandy, Aidan was introduced to strong liquor and after a number of accidents his football career was finally halted by a bad injury sustained on the field during a game. The loss of his dream hit Aidan badly, but by now Mandy had fallen for him in a big way and taken him under her wing. A near-death experience after getting involved with the rave scene and Ecstasy led Aidan to go home to Ireland in May and, surprisingly, Mandy followed him. She soon returned, however, having had a poor reception from Aidan's family. Aidan himself found that he no longer fitted in at home and, a few weeks later, he too returned to Walford, hoping to find Mandy and make a fresh start.

*Aidan and Mandy — young lovers who just didn't fit in.*

Reunited, the young lovers were unable to find work or accommodation and for a while they squatted in Pete's flat, and then later in the old squat at number 5. Mandy began 'clipping' to earn them spending money, but when Aidan found out exactly what this was—soliciting as a prostitute and then running away with the unsatisfied client's money—he made her promise to stop. They both found employment at the shop in Bridge Street for a few weeks, working for the latest manager, Mrs Andreos. When that job fell through they began to go into decline, with Aidan getting particularly depressed. Tricky Dicky purchased number 5 and evicted them, making them homeless in the weeks before Christmas. On Christmas Day Aidan decided to

commit suicide—and would have done but for the intervention of the powers-that-be at the BBC, who felt that a suicide on Christmas Day would be too depressing even for *EastEnders*. In the revised version Mandy arrived in time to stop Aidan jumping off a tower block, and the dejected youth went home to Ireland for good.

### And not forgetting...

Other stories saw the Mitchell brothers team up with Nigel to try to pull off a greyhound racing 'ringer' scam; Sharon becoming keen for Vicki to know the truth about her father; Nigel having his heart broken (more than once) by his new girlfriend Debbie; and Hattie being jilted by her fiancé Steve and miscarrying his baby. It also saw an unpre-

Faced with an imminent marriage to Hattie which he really didn't want to commit to, Steve jilted the poor girl and left Walford for the second time, not knowing that Hattie was pregnant with his child...

cedented pair of foreign trips—firstly a visit to France that was recorded with a little extra filming on the regular schedule and, secondly, a regular double-bank pair of episodes written and directed by the multitalented Tony McHale, set in Amsterdam.

## Comings 'n' Goings 1993

The beginning of 1993 saw the arrival of Sanjay (Deepak Verma) and Gita Kapoor (Shobu Kapoor), the first new regular Asian characters since the Karims had left in 1991. For the first time these Asian characters were Hindus not Moslems, and market traders, not the familiar stereotype of the Asian shopkeeper. We also made them old friends of Richard Cole, to help them, and him, blend into the Square. It had become clear that Richard was a man of few friends but, for dramatic reasons, he needed a confidante and Sanjay fulfilled that role.

Sanjay and Gita arrived in Albert Square in mid-story, living separately after the failure of their previous business. Sanjay needed to find a place for them to live, as Gita was pregnant. His weakness for gambling quickly became apparent and he needed the charity of Richard to secure a home. Once Sharmilla was born Gita became very tired and irritable. Meena, Gita's snobbish sister, came to visit and, despite her normal dislike of Sanjay, she began an affair with him. At the same time, in a state of post-natal depression, Gita was convinced that she was becoming paranoid as she suspected Sanjay of having an affair with Michelle.

> *Sanjay and Gita Kapoor came to Walford hoping a new baby might help them sort out their marital problems...*

## Some new arrivals...

January also saw the first appearance of Aidan (Sean Maguire), whose status as a teen pin-up put him in the Take That league by the end of the year. Although his length of service in *EastEnders* was relatively short, Aidan became a very popular character, particularly with the young audience, and Sean went on to develop his career by becoming a television presenter and singer. The initial

Aidan story also introduced Stan, coach of Walford Town's youth team, played by actor and writer Gawn Grainger.

Other new faces in 1993 included Debbie (Nicola Duffet) and her daughter Clare (Gemma Bissix), who arrived in Nigel's life in the summer. As ever, a never-ending stream of short-term characters appeared during 1993, such as Sylvia (Rachel Hiew), who worked at the café for a while; Danny Taurus (Billy Boyle) who tried to woo

Pauline; Nadia (Anna Barkan) who married Phil; Rose (Petra Markham) who fell fatally for Pete; and, finally, Clem (Jason Yates) and Russell (Ian Pepperall), two of Michelle's fellow students.

Gidea (Sian Martin) visited the Taverniers' household and proved to be part of the family—Jules' grand-daughter, from an affair he had had in Trinidad fifty years before. Despite this she became close to Clyde and, when she returned to the Caribbean, Clyde followed her and later decided to stay there. At the end of the year Hattie also left the programme, going for a Christmas visit to the family in Norwich never to return, as actress Michelle Gayle decided to develop her singing career.

### ... and a few farewells

Three major characters left during the year. The first was Pete, who went away with his new love Rose to start a new life which, sadly, was never to be. As I explained earlier, at one point the character of Pete Beale had been scheduled to die just after Christmas 1985 but he had managed to cheat death for a further eight years. Eventually, the writers felt that the character had reached a natural end. There was some talk of Pete and Kathy possibly getting back together again but it was felt that would have been a retrogressive step, and it was dismissed.

The second major character to leave was Dot Cotton. Actress June Brown felt that she had been in the programme for long enough and wanted a change. A loyal member of the cast for many years, June had a great deal of affection for the series and a passion

A grandmother after all — Dot with Nick and grandson Ashley.

for getting details right. Her farewell—sent to live with Nick and the family she had never known he had—was a reworking of a story that had been intended to give the character of Dot Cotton a new lease of life, by having her grandson Ashley come to live with her on the Square. The situation is open-ended, however, and Dot may yet be seen again, fag in hand, with a tomato juice, chatting in The Queen Vic.

The final long-running character who left during 1993 was Roly, the much passed-around poodle, who had found his way back home to The Vic and was once again

Sharon's dog. Entrusted by Grant to Mandy, of all people, Roly was reported to have been killed by a car. In truth, Roly the actor was getting a little too old to appear regularly on television and wanted to retire to live with his mistress, former producer and co-creator of *EastEnders*, Julia Smith. I am happy to report that at the time of writing Roly is alive and well. When I visited Julia to interview her for this book the first thing I heard was Roly barking a greeting!

Other characters who moved on during the year were Rachel, offered a chance to become a publisher's assistant, and Sam, whose marriage to Ricky had finally broken down after her introduction to the high life in the company of the Yuppie-like Clive. The year also saw the second exit by Steve

Elliot but, since like Frank Sinatra he always seems to make another comeback, perhaps we will list this as a temporary disappearance rather than a 'going'.

## A busy end to 1993

With all these changes, the last months of 1993 saw the beginnings of what would be a veritable stream of new characters, introduced in readiness for when three episodes a week would be broadcast. One new character, Auntie Nellie, made a brief appearance at Christmas at Pete Beale's funeral, as did a mysterious man who would later be revealed to be David Wicks. From November, we began to see six members of the Jacksons, an

A traditional East End send-off for a much-loved man. Pete Beale is laid to rest.

entirely new family. In a deliberate move to introduce the new family over a long period, the characters came and went from November onwards but didn't move into the Square until the following year. The complete family consists of Alan (Howard Anthony), Carol (Lindsey Coulson), Bianca (Patsy Palmer), Robbie (Dean Gaffney), Sonia (Natalie Cassidy) and Billy (Devon Anderson).

## Memorable Episodes 1993

### Episode 826 (21/1/93)

This was the last of three episodes which featured the long-awaited trial of Nick Cotton, all written by Tony Jordan. One of the interesting aspects of this was that none of the script editors or producers who had been responsible for the original episodes

The trial of Nick Cotton dramatized the legal process – we knew he'd done it but could murder be proved in a court of law?

in which Eddie had been killed were working on the programme any more. To present the story of Nick's trial the programme-makers themselves had to review the evidence and watch the episodes leading up to the death of Eddie. In the end, although it is clear that Nick *was* responsible for stabbing Eddie, it is not clear that this was murder. The jury's verdict: 'Not Guilty.'

### Episode 840 (11/3/93)

This was the second of two episodes by Susan Boyd, dominated by the kidnapping of Vicki and complicated by Michelle's involvement with the unstable Jack Woodman. Susan Tully's portrayal of a desperate mother was particularly outstanding.

### Episode 856 (6/5/93)

Written by Kolton Lee, this was the climax of the story of Aidan's drug experimentation, in which he ended up in hospital. The same episode saw the surprise conclusion to Pat's story when she was sent to prison for her driving offence.

### Episode 858 (13/5/93)

It was no accident that, as Pat went into prison, Grant was coming out. In this episode, written and directed by Tony McHale, Phil went to meet Grant after his release from prison and, finding him a changed man, decided not to tell him about his affair with Sharon. The secret remained buried, a bomb with a long fuse, primed to explode some time in the future.

The Mitchell boys, Phil and Grant, and the new face of the East End – London's Canary Wharf.

### Episode 861 (25/5/93)

It wasn't all doom and high drama in 1993. Episodes like this one, written by Tony Jordan, which featured Nigel's birthday party at Dot's house, brought much-needed humour to the programme and introduced Nigel to his future wife.

## Pick of the Year 1993

### Episode 892 (9/9/93)

September is always the target for big audience-grabbing episodes. To coincide with the start of the BBC's 1993 autumn season the programme pulled out all the stops and it is Episode 892, written by Tony McHale and transmitted on 9 September 1993, which I have chosen as Pick of the Year. Ever since the decision had been made for

Arthur to have an affair it was inevitable that, at some point, Pauline would find out. The way this could happen was the subject of much discussion at a number of story conferences; should Pauline work it out for herself or should some third party tell her the truth? In the end it was felt that Arthur should decide to tell her himself. Episode 891 climaxed with Arthur doing just that.

Episode 892 picked up directly and was dominated by the aftermath of Arthur's confession. Over the years Wendy Richard and Bill Treacher have played many, many rows as Pauline and Arthur but this was something new, an act of betrayal on a massive scale. The row turned violent—Pauline hit Arthur with a frying pan and Arthur was only saved from further humiliation by the arrival of Gita and Sanjay, who had left Sharmilla with Pauline while they went out. Arthur tried hard to persuade Pauline that their marriage was worth fighting for, but when Mrs Hewitt kept ringing

Pauline faces Christine Hewitt over the photo that she gave to Arthur. Her confrontation with Arthur was less genteel.

and Pauline worked out that it was she who had bought their new portable television, she lost her temper again. She threw the television at Arthur and chucked him out of the house. It seemed that the most solid of *EastEnders'* marriages, one of the bedrocks of the series, was over.

Written by Tony McHale, who as story consultant had a major hand in shaping the development of the on-going stories at the time, and directed by newcomer Keith Boak, the episode was a classic half-hour of drama, Albert Square-style.

# 1994:

# That Was the Year That . . .

This was a historic year for *EastEnders*—and a new beginning, as from April the programme was given three episodes every week. In previous years when *Brookside*, *Coronation Street* and *Eldorado* had appeared three times a week there had always been speculation that, one day, *EastEnders* would follow but at Elstree such talk was always dismissed. People thought it would be impossible to maintain *EastEnders'* high standard of writing, acting and production with the increased pressure of a third weekly episode. In 1994 the programme-makers were given the challenge of proving these doubters wrong.

When the decision to go for an extra episode was made it was decided to mark the new era by restarting the episode numbering at 1. The last twice-weekly episode (Episode 952) went out on Thursday 7 April 1994, and the following Monday, 11 April at 8.00 p.m. saw *EastEnders'* second 'Episode 1' begin.

Having set-up the transition to the new schedule the first trio of episodes marked the departure from the programme of Leonard Lewis. Barbara Emile became the new series producer and was given the task of taking *EastEnders* on into a new era, along with producers Diana Kyle and Jane Fallon.

At the time of writing, transmission of three episodes of *EastEnders* every week has just started, and the stories for the rest of the year are still being written and planned. For 1994, therefore, it is impossible to write a 'That Was the Year That' chapter in quite the same way as I have for the earlier years. Instead I will look at some of the storylines presented in the early months of the year . . .

## Problems for Sanjay

The year began strongly with Gita's discovery of Sanjay's affair with Meena, his sister-in-law, and she immediately threw her cheating husband out. When she discovered that Sanjay would have rights to see his daughter Sharmilla, Gita took her child and left Walford. A few months later she returned and took possession of the flat again.

Sanjay's affair kept things in the family – he had a foolish fling with Gita's sister Meena.

With the couple sharing the work on the stall and the care of Sharmilla, Sanjay began to think that it would only be a matter of time before he and Gita would be back together. But with Meena still visiting Gita in an effort to be reconciled with her, it was not going to be easy. In the meantime Sanjay was forced to find accommodation elsewhere in the Square.

## Ian bounces back

Ian began the year working for his mother at the café but when Phil proved to her that he was using it as a basis for his own freelance work for the Meal Machine, she fired him. With the twins, Lucy and Pete, Steven and Cindy to feed, for a while things looked bleak for Ian but with his usual ingenuity he bounced back with a new venture—Ian Beale

December saw the birth of their twins, Pete and Lucy, and things seemed to be picking up for Ian and Cindy. However going on past history, Cindy may not be happy to spend the rest of her life as just a mother of three . . .

Finance. A loan shark by any other name, the new business gave employment to Ricky – who was not cut out to be a heavy. And while Ian's popularity with the locals plummeted, as more and more of them began to owe him money, Cindy began to feel trapped and ignored by her husband.

## Happiness for Kathy?

Meanwhile Kathy and Phil's relationship developed through 1994, and early in the year they began to live together. In March Kathy was angry with Phil when he purchased Frank's share of the café for her. Later in the year Kathy began to have nightmares about Willmott-Brown, leading Phil to go in search of him. After he discovered that Willmott-Brown was in prison for committing another rape, Phil's relationship with Kathy hit another bump when she learned that he had been responsible for setting fire to Frank's car lot and killing the vagrant

who was there at the time. Despite all this, Phil loves Kathy and in time the idea of marriage was mentioned. The only problem is that Phil was already married, of course . . .

## Drama at the Vic

The Vic was the scene of much drama at the beginning of the year when Grant began to show signs of reverting to type. His disastrous involvement with Dougie Briggs, which led to the shooting of Michelle, was only the beginning. A little while later he came out the worse in a fight with some heavies that Phil had got involved with at the Arches, and a few weeks after that he punched David Wicks, after accusing him of chatting up Sharon. Meanwhile one of the results of Michelle's stay in hospital was that Vicki got to learn that she was Sharon's half-sister, when Sharon told her. When Michelle found out it caused a rift between the two women that was to last for some

As *EastEnders* built up to going out three times a week, Grant's old army pal Dougie Briggs arrived at The Vic. Despite Sharon's reservations about him, Grant insisted that his mate was okay and even began planning a criminal 'job' with him. When Grant discovered that Dougie had a shotgun, things began to look more worrying . . .

time. When Phil and Kathy begin to talk about marriage, Sharon realized that her feelings for Phil hadn't exactly gone away ... As the autumn of 1994 arrived the long-buried secret at the Vic seemed to be working towards the surface...

## Life goes on for the Fowlers

For Michelle the early part of the year was dominated by her flat-mate leaving and the horror of the siege and the injuries she sustained that night. The first problem was solved when Mark decided to move in with her but the other took longer to deal with. One result was that her finals at University suffered and this brought her into contact with her personal tutor, Geoff Barnes. The summer brought her final results—a third—and a new relationship, with Geoff.

Pauline and Arthur began the year continuing the healing process that had begun at Christmas. At first Arthur slept alone but after the family was successful in persuading Ian and David to sell the stall to Mark, Pauline accepted Arthur back into her bed. The affair with Mrs Hewitt was not forgotten, especially now that their new lodger Auntie Nellie has found out about it, but at least Arthur and Pauline could begin to rebuild their marriage.

## The Jacksons move in

The beginning of 1994 saw the Jackson family complete their arrival when they moved from the tower block into Dot's old house. A few months later they were joined by Blossom, Alan's granny. Alan got himself odd bits of work on Mark's stall, and later

The Jacksons – a classic 'problem' family. Or are they just prone to bad luck?

as a mechanic for the new car lot/garage operation jointly run by David and Ricky. Bianca had a brief affair with Richard Cole until he grew bored with her when, encouraged by her mate Natalie, she took her revenge, stole the number of Tricky's credit card and ran up a huge bill on it. When David Wicks began chatting up Bianca, Carol told Pat the truth about Bianca's father—that he was David. Pat refused to believe her, but when Carol told David the news, he realized that it was the truth.

## Nightmare for Pat

The Butchers began the year badly, with financial problems of great magnitude. Frank

managed to sell the old flat to Phil—but for much less than he had been asking—and then later sold him his share of the café. Despite these transactions Frank was still in deep trouble. Finally, in desperation, he arranged with Phil to have the car lot burnt, so he could claim on the insurance. When that went wrong—and a homeless boy died—Frank went to pieces and, at the beginning of April, he left the Square without warning.

For Pat, not knowing where Frank was, or even if he were alive or dead, the following few months were a nightmare. Finally after a visit from Diane, who Frank had been to visit, Pat started to accept that he was gone for good and began getting on with life. Ricky and David teamed up to re-open the car lot under the new name of Deals For Wheels.

**Time to move on?** Frank Butcher realized that his money problems were not going to go away so he decided to go away himself instead.

## Return of a familiar face

February saw the unexpected return of Steve Elliot, who seems to have picked up Rod Norman's habit of bouncing back to Walford. Not knowing what had happened to Hattie after his departure, he returned wanting to make things up to her. When he went to Norwich to see her he found Etta, who inadvertently told him the truth—that Hattie had been pregnant and had miscarried the baby. Back in Walford Steve was soon pursuing a new dream, as a partner to Della in a new hairdressing salon. With hopes of becoming more than just a business partner to Della, Steve was shocked and slightly horrified to discover that she preferred to share her bed with her girlfriend, Binnie.

## Wedding bells

It's often said that happiness is a rare commodity in Walford but 1994 saw one happy couple. Nigel and Debbie finally got their act together in March when Debbie decided, at last, to choose Nigel instead of Liam. Within a couple of months they were sharing a flat in George Street and Nigel got himself a permanent, respectable job, managing the video shop in Turpin Road. Troublesome Liam moved into a bedsit in the Square but, despite his presence, Debbie and Nigel went ahead with their wedding plans and married in July. Defeated, Liam gave up his attempts to gain custody of Clare and Debbie and Nigel appeared to have a happy future, except that Nigel had paid for the wedding by borrowing money from Ian's company, Ian Beale Finance . . .

## Looking ahead

One of the wonderful things about EastEnders is how it grows. A little moment between characters in one script can develop into a major storyline years later. A reference to someone made casually in one episode might lead to that character becoming a regular in years to come. Despite producers and writers projecting into the future, making plans for characters, splitting couples up, bringing others together, at the end of the day the future remains unknown.

Writing now, there may be huge storylines that dominate the end of 1994 that I can't know about. Maybe we'll just have to wait until 2005 and the twentieth anniversary before someone can really look back at 1994 and say 'That Was the Year That . . .'

## Comings 'n' Goings 1994

With the new programme frequency it was inevitable that there would be new characters, and the process of increasing the size of the regular cast began towards the end of 1993 with the introduction of the Jacksons. This process continued into the new year as Natalie Price (Lucy Speed), Bianca's best mate, started to be seen hanging around and then, a little later, Alan's grandmother Blossom (Mona Hammond) came to live with the Jacksons.

## New faces and a few familiar ones

Two characters who had made their debut at Pete's funeral at Christmas returned to the show for longer runs. Auntie Nellie (Elizabeth Kelly), a relative of Lou's, came to live with the Fowlers, much to the horror

of Arthur who found her to be an interfering old lady, reminiscent of Lou at her worst. Pat's first son, David Wicks (Michael French), came to live in Walford, apparently wanting to make up for the years he had been away. In truth he was on the run from debts and from paying maintenance to a wife and two kids. He soon proved to be a sly operator, with an inability to tell the complete truth about things. No sooner had he arrived than he was trying to make money out of his share of Pete's stall. When he learned that Bianca Jackson was in fact his child, from a school-day affair with Carol, David was hurt that Pat had kept this information from him and left, but he was soon back, in debt, and desperate again.

March saw the arrival of Della Alexander (Michelle Joseph),

**Pat Wicks with her first born son David — a chance to make up for the lost years, or just the latest man who will try to take advantage of her? Time will tell.**

**Steve bounced back with a new plan to make his fortune, this time using the hairdressing skills of Della Alexander.**

who initially appeared to be designed to be the new love interest for Steve Elliot. In fact, Della's story was more complicated and required the arrival of another new character, Binnie Roberts (Sophie Langham), before it could be played out. Della and Binnie were the first lesbian couple to be featured in *EastEnders*, and follow in the tradition of previous positive examples of characters who just happen to be gay.

The year also introduced Geoff Barnes (David Roper), a lecturer at the University Michelle was attending. For the first time since Den, Michelle found herself attracted to a much older man. After years of disastrous relationships with men, who can say if she has made the right choice this time? The year also saw new love for Michelle's brother, Mark. Ironically Mark met his new girlfriend as a result of being HIV positive—they met in a hospice where they were both visiting friends dying from Aids.

There were also a number of visitors from the past in 1994. Nadia, Phil's wife, appeared in the summer, when she forced Phil to help her again in return for agreeing to a divorce. Etta paid a visit during March to collect Hattie's things and to try to persuade Jules to leave Walford too. June saw a visit from Diane Butcher, who came to give Pat a final message from Frank.

## Some farewells

Mention of Frank brings us on to characters who left Walford during 1994. The most significant of them all was Frank Butcher.

Racked with guilt after a vagrant died in the fire at the car lot, and finally faced with financial problems beyond his ability to duck and dive, Frank disappeared at the beginning of April. Only time will tell if the character will ever be able to return.

March saw the departure of Shelley who, rejected by Mark, decided that she couldn't carry on living with Michelle and seeing Mark every day at the market. Finally, Tricky Dicky—the man everyone loves to hate—fled from Walford in July, when his old adversary Ian Beale managed to get the upper hand by delving into Tricky's past.

The latter months of the year will bring more comings and goings, as the story of *EastEnders* unfolds three times a week.

## Memorable Episodes/Pick of the Year 1994

When I came to review some of the earlier years it was relatively easy to select the highlight episodes and to find a 'Pick of the Year'. In the more recent years it has become much harder, not because of any change in the standard of writing but because the episodes are too recent. Only with the benefit of hindsight can one really judge which were the really special episodes. The situation is not helped by the fact that over the last couple of years I have joined the ranks of the *EastEnders* writers myself, and trying to select the best episodes by my colleagues is an additional headache.

The other problem with selecting the best of 1994 is that, as I am writing these words, episodes for 1994 are still being made, some are still being written and some have yet to be commissioned.

Nevertheless there is one episode which I think I can suggest, even now, to be the Pick of the Year: Episode 41 (12/7/94) by Debbie Cook. As the one thousandth episode of *EastEnders* this was always going to be special, but Series Producer Barbara Emile decided to mark the occasion with an on-screen celebration. The episode was dominated by the summer wedding of Nigel and Debbie—a happy day, helped by the fact that Grant and Phil made sure that Debbie's ex-husband Liam could not spoil things.

Typically even while Debbie and Nigel finally found happiness, matters between Phil and Kathy were reaching a new low. With the up-front story of the wedding, and the other characters' stories slipped in as well, this was a classic example of what makes *EastEnders* a very special television serial. Or even (say it quietly) as a soap!

1,000 episodes and still going strong. Cameo appearances by Ethel Skinner and Dr Legg provided a hint of nostalgia, but the episode was dominated by the wedding of relative newcomers Nigel and Debbie and a good old-fashioned *EastEnders* street party.

# Behind the Scenes in Albert Square

In the summer of 1993 a decision was made by Alan Yentob, the new controller of BBC1, to add a third episode of *EastEnders* every week to his schedule, beginning as soon as possible. This led to great changes in the way the programme is made, as the massive machine which produces *EastEnders* had to be redesigned and re-equipped to provide the required extra weekly episode. In addition the new system had to be developed whilst simultaneously maintaining the current output of two episodes every week.

The process that brings three episodes of *EastEnders* to your screens every week is a complex and long one and the full story of how the programme is made would fill a book on its own, but to give an idea of how it is done this section will trace the process that leads from story conference to the finished episode.

## The story conference

The first stage for any story in *EastEnders* is the story conference, a brain-storming meeting, held every two-and-a-half months. Before each conference, series script editor Louise Berridge contacts all the *EastEnders*

writers to ask for new story ideas. She includes a state-of-play document which tells the writers exactly what each of the characters has been up to in the latest episodes that have been commissioned, and points out which of them are most in need of new stories. Over the next few weeks, the writers submit their stories and a large reading document is assembled.

The conference itself takes place over two days, a Sunday and a Monday, in a hotel not far from the Elstree Studios. At the conference the producers, script editors and a representative selection of the regular writers work their way through a discussion of each of the submitted stories and all the characters. They go to the hotel, away from the office, in order to minimize interruptions—the meetings can easily run over as it is, and if they happened at the Elstree offices they would probably last all week!

When stories have been agreed Louise then breaks down the progression of the stories into the individual episodes, ready for the next stage—commissioning scripts.

## Commissioning the scripts

Episodes are commissioned over two meetings, on successive Mondays; first, there is a planning meeting at which the general outlines for a set of twelve episodes are discussed, and then there is a commissioning meeting at which the writers firm up what they will be covering in each episode.

At the planning meeting the writers who have been chosen to write this batch of episodes talk through the stories that will be covered with the producers and script

editors. Problems of plot and characterization are mentioned, and after a long morning the writers go away to plan their episodes in greater detail.

The second half of the commissioning process is the commissioning meeting. Here the floor is given to each writer, who tells the meeting what he or she would like to do with their episode or episodes. At this meeting the hard decisions about which characters are available, and which sets can be used, have to be made. Often a writer will not know exactly how a particular plot strand will be achieved until they actually sit down to write it—on these occasions they will resort to the phrase 'in a clever and amusing way to be invented by the writer'—a long-running EastEnders writers' joke.

### Writing the scripts

The writers then have four weeks, on average, in which to write the first draft of their episode(s). This is the lonely stage of writing, as each writer wrestles with the logistical limitations while trying to write the best dramatic material they can. There are two main elements to the task; first there is the skill of structuring the episodes to advance all the stories through the episode and, second, there is the creative art of bringing all of the characters alive within those stories.

When the scripts are delivered they are quickly photocopied and circulated to the people who need to see them—the relevant producer and the script editors. Comments are gathered, continuity notes marked and the script editor then discusses the scripts in detail with the producer. After this meeting the script editor will have a meeting with the writer to discuss re-writes. The job of script editor is a peculiar one, part-editor, part-diplomat. It takes a special skill to give a writer notes that mean he or she will have to re-write almost all of their script while not destroying the writer's confidence!

Due to the complex continuity on a programme like EastEnders changes are always needed to a first draft and normally further changes are needed before a final draft of the script can be prepared and printed. At this stage the script enters production.

### Going into production

Each week's episodes are produced by a production team that consists of a director, production manager, production assistant and an assistant floor manager. The director is responsible for the dramatic interpretation of the script, for the camera-scripting of the recording and for overseeing the post-production of the episodes. The production manager is responsible for scheduling and running all the technical aspects of the episodes and for controlling the floor during recording. In the world of independent television he or she would be called a first assistant director. The production assistant is responsible for the paperwork, administration and continuity. The assistant floor manager is, as the name implies, an assistant on the floor, responsible for props, rehearsal schedules and liaison with actors. The production team is assisted by other specialized programme departments whose personnel, such as designers, costume designers, make-

up designers and prop buyers, work on a longer run of episodes. One of the first of these to begin work on any new set of scripts is the location manager.

The art of location-finding for *EastEnders* is very specialized, as it tries to match the needs of the script with the physical reality of actual locations, while always being limited by the need for the locations to be as close to the Elstree base as possible.

While locations are being finalized, the production team begins work recording the programme's lot material. Two days are now available on the lot for every trio of episodes, and these are normally the first Monday and Wednesday of the recording schedule.

## Recording the episodes

Recording on the lot is very efficient, and the crews regularly record up to twelve minutes of material in one day. The only problem with the lot is that it tends to be quite cold—as actors who spend a lot of time recording outdoor scenes will tell you! There is no time in the busy schedule for the lot material to be rehearsed—although there is usually a rehearsal if a particularly heavy scene is to be played on the lot—so the actors have to be extra alert to take in the director's instructions. Time is valuable—and poor planning of the lot can waste a lot of time.

The location work is also recorded in the same week as the lot material, normally one day for each trio of episodes. Location work tends to deal with one strand in any given episode, and focus on a small number of characters. It also offers one of the few perks

for the hardworking souls who work on the programme, as they often get to enjoy the joys of location catering. The canteen at Elstree is very good, but there is something special about a hot meal, served from a kitchen in the back of a van, which you eat on a coach!

There are rehearsals for the material to be recorded in the two *EastEnders* studios. On the fifth and sixth floors of Neptune House, the six-storey block of office buildings at the far end of the Elstree site, are the two rehearsal rooms used by the programme. Here the shapes of the regular and guest sets are marked out in coloured tape on the floor, the furniture represented by mock-ups and copies. A hardboard replica of the Vic's bar dominates the top end of the fifth-floor room, as it has done since the first rehearsals here at the end of 1984. The surfaces of the bar are covered with graffiti, much of it unprintable, the handiwork of bored actors waiting to rehearse. Some of the graffiti is obscure: 'I've got a brand new combine harvester'; some more obvious: 'I wish I was in Neighbours'; and some is just a variation on 'Kilroy was here'.

The busy *EastEnders* schedule means that rehearsals have to be fitted in around the actual recordings. On the days that one week's episodes are being rehearsed, another week's are being recorded. Inevitably actors find themselves rushing from studio to rehearsals and then back to the studio; also inevitably the construction of a timetable for rehearsals, working out exactly when all the artistes needed for any scene might be available, is a nightmare. Often the assistant

floor manager is required to read in the lines of missing actors, normally to the amusement of the real actors.

On the Tuesday of the second week of production there are two final rehearsals of all the studio material. The first is called the technical run and is a rehearsal of the scenes in the order that they will be recorded. This allows the technical staff, the camera crew, sound crew, etc., to anticipate and solve problems before the actual recording. The second rehearsal is called the producer's run—and this is a final run of the scenes in story order, at which the director shows the producer how the scenes will be played and shot. For the writer, script editor and producer it is a chance to see a dress rehearsal of the action, to make final adjustments to lines or performances, and to make sure that the director is getting what was intended out of the scripts. This is also the point at which an accurate timing for the episode can be made. Each episode of the programme should last 27 minutes and 15 seconds, and if the timing of the episodes is wrong after the producer's run then material has to be cut or sometimes added before recording begins on the Thursday.

During studio recording the director sits in the gallery alongside a vision mixer, the production assistant and the resources co-ordinator who is in charge of technical operations. On the floor each scene is rehearsed, both for the actors and the technicians. The camera operators follow a pre-prepared list of shots, as planned by the director, in the camera script. When the scene has been run a couple of times a recording is attempted. As the production assistant calls off the shots, as each cutting point comes up in the script, the vision mixer cuts between the various camera angles, timing the cuts to minimize the distraction to the eye. Like the videotape editor, the vision mixer is concerned with making the transition between separate shots as unnoticeable as possible.

## The post-production process

With the recording finished the episodes move into post-production. All the recorded material is sent to the videotape editor, who will already have received the material that has been shot on location at the lot and cut it together. Now, using the director's notes about which takes and shots he or she particularly wants to use, the videotape editor can begin the job of assembling the complete programme.

Once upon a time, all the editing of *EastEnders* went on in the editing suites at Television Centre. Now there is a state-of-the-art set of suites at Elstree itself, constantly serving the daily needs of *Newsroom South East* and the weekly needs of *Top of the Pops* and *EastEnders*. Here in VT edit suites, packed with more high-tech equipment than the bridge of the Starship Enterprise, each episode of *EastEnders* is finally assembled.

After the recording has finished the director will work with VHS copies of all the material, marked with computerized time-code to identify each frame of tape, and make detailed notes of exactly which of the various takes of each scene he or she wants to use.

In the editing suite the videotape editor can often spot problems that were not immediately apparent, such as a close-up which won't cut into the scene because the actor's hands are in the wrong place. Once this edit has been done the tapes are sent to the relevant producer for checking, and the producer will usually ask for some changes to be made.

The first edit is cut for the story rather than to time; the adjustments to make each episode the right length can then be made at the second edit. With the new D3 videotape, which is now the standard in broadcast television, the old problem of signal deterioration each time the image is copied to another tape has disappeared—the picture signal on D3 tape is digital and there is no loss of picture quality at all.

With the visual editing complete, the next stage of post-production is the sypher dub, at which the sound is completed. The raw sound that was recorded is mixed and added to background noise: train sounds, market sounds, background radios, juke-box music ... Trains are particularly important—the illusion of the railway bridge in Bridge Street is maintained almost entirely with sound effects and only once has a train been seen on the bridge. With the dub complete, the programmes have a final technical review to ensure that the finished product meets the exacting technical standards for broadcast by the BBC, then the episodes are viewed by the current head of series and serials, Michael Wearing.

The next time the episodes are viewed, an average of 16 million people will be watching ... as another episode of the BBC's most popular drama reaches its audience.

Meanwhile, back at Elstree, stories are coming in for the next story conference, as the writers and producers begin thinking about what will be hitting the screen in eight months' time ...

**Recording in the studio, Stage One, at Elstree. A scene between Michelle and Dougie for the second Episode 1 is rehearsed on set before being recorded on videotape.**

# The Future of *EastEnders*

Ten years is a long time in television—and the achievement of *EastEnders* in reaching that milestone should not be underestimated. The programme is still, however, younger than other regular serials such as *Brookside*, *Emmerdale* and *Coronation Street*.

The future of *EastEnders* is a blank page. As the century comes to an end television will be going through immense changes. In 1996 the BBC's Charter is up for renewal and some commentators think that the BBC as the institution it is today, is doomed.

If the BBC does continue, and if *EastEnders* is still around in another ten years (or perhaps twenty), what kind of programme will it be? By the twentieth anniversary will we be watching it on flat-screen televisions hanging on our living-room walls? Will it be transmitted in 3-D? Who can say?

Crystal-ball gazing is a risky game, and it would take a braver man than me to attempt it. In any case it has already been done. During the *Children in Need Appeal* of 1993 the BBC produced a special two-part edition of the long-running Science Fiction programme *Dr Who*, part of which was shot on the Albert Square lot at Elstree. A scene from it, set in the future, showed grey-haired Pauline Fowler and Kathy Beale (or Mit-

Kathy and Pauline circa the 21st century with third Doctor, (Jon Pertwee) and Pudsey the *Children in Need* bear.

chell, perhaps, by then), selling fruit and veg from a replica of Mark's current stall, the produce priced with barcodes.

One thing that is certain (as far as anything can be certain in the world of television) is that Den and Angie will not be coming back to *EastEnders*. With one of the characters firmly established as dead and the other equally firmly enjoying a new life in Florida, Den and Angie will not be back behind the bar at The Queen Vic. As for other major characters who have left the series, anything is possible—except for those whose characters have died, of course.

One of the interesting things that will happen over the next ten years and beyond will be the gradual ageing of the regular members of the cast, if they stay with the programme. For example, by the time the twentieth anniversary rolls along in 2005, all of the children will be much older; Martin Fowler will be twenty, Vicki will be nineteen, Janine Butcher twenty, Steven Beale fifteen and Sharmilla Kapoor twelve.

For all that I can't know—yet—about the future of *EastEnders*, there are *some* things that I can be sure about. While *EastEnders* continues to be made by men and women who care passionately about honest, popular drama, it will carry on being one of Britain's most successful television programmes. And come the end of the millennium, as we all enter the twenty-first century, you can bet that there will be a massive party down at the Vic and, in the midst of the joy and laughter, someone will be having a crisis, finding out a secret or betraying a loved one. Life's like that—and so is *EastEnders*!

**EastEnders**
**THE FIRST 10 YEARS**

# Episode Listings

| Episode | Transmission date | Writer | Director |
|---|---|---|---|
| 1 | 19/02/85 | Gerry Huxham | Matthew Robinson |
| 2 | 21/02/85 | Jane Hollowood | Matthew Robinson |
| 3 | 26/02/85 | Valerie Georgeson | Vivienne Cozens |
| 4 | 28/02/85 | Bill Lyons | Vivienne Cozens |
| 5 | 05/03/85 | Jane Hollowood | Peter Edwards |
| 6 | 07/03/85 | Jane Hollowood | Peter Edwards |
| 7 | 12/03/85 | Gerry Huxham | Matthew Robinson |
| 8 | 14/03/85 | Gerry Huxham | Matthew Robinson |
| 9 | 19/03/85 | Rosemary Mason | Sue Butterworth |
| 10 | 21/03/85 | Jim Hawkins | Sue Butterworth |
| 11 | 26/03/85 | Jim Hawkins | Peter Edwards |
| 12 | 28/03/85 | Gilly Fraser | Peter Edwards |
| 13 | 02/04/85 | Michael Robartes | Matthew Robinson |
| 14 | 04/04/85 | Valerie Georgeson | Matthew Robinson |
| 15 | 09/04/85 | Bill Lyons | Sue Butterworth |
| 16 | 11/04/85 | Glen McCoy | Sue Butterworth |
| 17 | 16/04/85 | Christopher Russell | Peter Edwards |
| 18 | 18/04/85 | Bill Lyons | Peter Edwards |
| 19 | 23/04/85 | Valerie Georgeson | Malcolm Taylor |
| 20 | 25/04/85 | Michael Robartes | Malcolm Taylor |
| 21 | 30/04/85 | Frances Galleymore | Jeremy Ancock |
| 22 | 02/05/85 | Bill Lyons | Jeremy Ancock |
| 23 | 07/05/85 | Bev Doyle | Sue Butterworth |
| 24 | 09/05/85 | Valerie Georgeson | Sue Butterworth |
| 25 | 14/05/85 | Jane Hollowood | Malcolm Taylor |
| 26 | 16/05/85 | Juliet Ace | Malcolm Taylor |
| 27 | 21/05/85 | Bill Lyons | Jeremy Ancock |
| 28 | 23/05/85 | Tony Dennis | Jeremy Ancock |
| 29 | 28/05/85 | Bill Lyons | Sue Butterworth |
| 30 | 30/05/85 | Tony McHale | Sue Butterworth |
| 31 | 04/06/85 | Rosemary Mason | Malcolm Taylor |
| 32 | 06/06/85 | Valerie Georgeson | Malcolm Taylor |
| 33 | 11/06/85 | Bill Lyons | Jeremy Ancock |
| 34 | 13/06/85 | Jim Hawkins | Jeremy Ancock |
| 35 | 18/06/85 | Harry Duffin | Sue Butterworth |
| 36 | 20/06/85 | Jane Hollowood | Sue Butterworth |
| 37 | 25/06/85 | Gilly Fraser | Brian Morgan |
| 38 | 27/06/85 | Michael Robartes | Brian Morgan |
| 39 | 02/07/85 | Jane Hollowood | Matthew Robinson |
| 40 | 04/07/85 | Glen McCoy | Matthew Robinson |
| 41 | 09/07/85 | Gerry Huxham | Antonia Bird |
| 42 | 11/07/85 | Bill Lyons | Antonia Bird |
| 43 | 16/07/85 | Valerie Georgeson | Brian Morgan |
| 44 | 18/07/85 | Liane Aukin | Brian Morgan |
| 45 | 23/07/85 | Rosemary Mason | Matthew Robinson |
| 46 | 25/07/85 | Michael Robartes | Matthew Robinson |
| 47 | 30/07/85 | John Crisp | Antonia Bird |
| 48 | 01/08/85 | Jane Hollowood | Antonia Bird |
| 49 | 06/08/85 | Valerie Georgeson | Brian Morgan |
| 50 | 08/08/85 | Peter Batt | Brian Morgan |
| 51 | 13/08/85 | Bill Lyons | Matthew Robinson |
| 52 | 15/08/85 | Bev Doyle | Matthew Robinson |
| 53 | 20/08/85 | Michael Robartes | Antonia Bird |
| 54 | 22/08/85 | Jane Hollowood | Antonia Bird |
| 55 | 27/08/85 | Gilly Fraser | Stephen Butcher |
| 56 | 29/08/85 | Tony McHale | Stephen Butcher |
| 57 | 03/09/85 | Rosemary Mason | Mike Gibbon |
| 58 | 05/09/85 | Billy Hamon | Mike Gibbon |
| 59 | 10/09/85 | Bill Lyons | Robert Gabriel |
| 60 | 12/09/85 | Juliet Ace | Robert Gabriel |
| 61 | 17/09/85 | Chris Anstis | Stephen Butcher |
| 62 | 19/09/85 | Bill Lyons | Stephen Butcher |
| 63 | 24/09/85 | Jane Hollowood | Mike Gibbon |
| 64 | 26/09/85 | Valerie Georgeson | Mike Gibbon |
| 65 | 01/10/85 | Bill Lyons | Julia Smith |
| 66 | 03/10/85 | Tony Holland | Julia Smith |
| 67 | 08/10/85 | Jane Hollowood | Stephen Butcher |
| 68 | 10/10/85 | Charlie Humphreys | Stephen Butcher |
| 69 | 15/10/85 | Tony McHale | Mike Gibbon |
| 70 | 17/10/85 | Chris Anstis | Mike Gibbon |
| 71 | 22/10/85 | Peter Batt | Robert Gabriel |
| 72 | 24/10/85 | Harry Duffin | Robert Gabriel |
| 73 | 29/10/85 | Michael Robartes | Antonia Bird |
| 74 | 31/10/85 | Bill Lyons | Antonia Bird |
| 75 | 05/11/85 | Liane Aukin | William Slater |
| 76 | 07/11/85 | Jane Hollowood | William Slater |
| 77 | 12/11/85 | Gilly Fraser | Chris Clough |
| 78 | 14/11/85 | Tony McHale | Chris Clough |
| 79 | 19/11/85 | Allan Swift | Antonia Bird |
| 80 | 21/11/85 | Rosemary Mason | Antonia Bird |
| 81 | 26/11/85 | Gerry Huxham | William Slater |
| 82 | 28/11/85 | Susan Boyd | William Slater |
| 83 | 03/12/85 | Hugh Miller | Chris Clough |
| 84 | 05/12/85 | Michael Robartes | Chris Clough |
| 85 | 10/12/85 | Bill Lyons | Antonia Bird |
| 86 | 12/12/85 | Jane Hollowood | Antonia Bird |
| 87 | 17/12/85 | David Ashton | William Slater |
| 88 | 19/12/85 | Rosemary Mason | William Slater |
| 89 | 24/12/85 | Jim Hawkins | Chris Clough |

| Episode | Transmission date | Writer | Director |
|---------|-------------------|--------|----------|
| 90 | 26/12/85 | Tony McHale | Chris Clough |
| 91 | 31/12/85 | Bill Lyons | Julia Smith |
| 92 | 02/01/86 | Bill Lyons | Julia Smith |
| 93 | 07/01/86 | Bev Doyle | Sue Butterworth |
| 94 | 09/01/86 | Peter Batt | Sue Butterworth |
| 95 | 14/01/86 | Juliet Ace | Mike Lloyd |
| 96 | 16/01/86 | Jane Hollowood | Mike Lloyd |
| 97 | 21/01/86 | Rosemary Mason | Robert Gabriel |
| 98 | 23/01/86 | Michael Robartes | Robert Gabriel |
| 99 | 28/01/86 | Bill Lyons | Sue Butterworth |
| 100 | 30/01/86 | Guido Casale | Sue Butterworth |
| 101 | 04/02/86 | Jane Hollowood | Mike Lloyd |
| 102 | 06/02/86 | David Hopkins | Mike Lloyd |
| 103 | 11/02/86 | Bill Lyons | Matthew Robinson |
| 104 | 13/02/86 | Charlie Humphreys | Matthew Robinson |
| 105 | 18/02/86 | Michael Robartes | Sue Butterworth |
| 106 | 20/02/86 | Liane Aukin | Sue Butterworth |
| 107 | 25/02/86 | Rosemary Mason | Mike Lloyd |
| 108 | 27/02/86 | Julia Schofield | Mike Lloyd |
| 109 | 04/03/86 | Glen McCoy | Matthew Robinson |
| 110 | 06/03/86 | Bill Lyons | Matthew Robinson |
| 111 | 11/03/86 | Tony McHale | Peter Moffat |
| 112 | 13/03/86 | Jane Hollowood | Peter Moffat |
| 113 | 18/03/86 | John Oakden | Tony Virgo |
| 114 | 20/03/86 | Rosemary Mason | Tony Virgo |
| 115 | 25/03/86 | Tony McHale | Kay Patrick |
| 116 | 27/03/86 | Bev Doyle | Kay Patrick |
| 117 | 01/04/86 | Jane Hollowood | Tony Virgo |
| 118 | 03/04/86 | Gilly Fraser | Tony Virgo |
| 119 | 08/04/86 | Bill Lyons | Peter Moffat |
| 120 | 10/04/86 | John Barrington | Peter Moffat |
| 121 | 15/04/86 | Michael Robartes | Kay Patrick |
| 122 | 17/04/86 | Tony McHale | Matthew Robinson |
| 123 | 22/04/86 | Peter Batt | Peter Moffat |
| 124 | 24/04/86 | Tony Bilbow | Peter Moffat |
| 125 | 29/04/86 | Liane Aukin | Tony Virgo |
| 126 | 01/05/86 | Jane Hollowood | Tony Virgo |
| 127 | 06/05/86 | Bill Lyons | Chris Clough |
| 128 | 08/05/86 | Guido Casale | Chris Clough |
| 129 | 13/05/86 | Charlie Humphreys | Ron Craddock |
| 130 | 15/05/86 | Peter Batt | Ron Craddock |
| 131 | 20/05/86 | Michael Robartes | Mike Gibbon |
| 132 | 22/05/86 | Rosemary Mason | Mike Gibbon |
| 133 | 27/05/86 | Jane Hollowood | Garth Tucker |
| 134 | 29/05/86 | Al Hunter | Garth Tucker |
| 135 | 03/06/86 | Tony McHale | Ron Craddock |
| 136 | 05/06/86 | Bill Lyons | Ron Craddock |
| 137 | 10/06/86 | Michael Robartes | Mike Gibbon |
| 138 | 12/06/86 | Juliet Ace | Mike Gibbon |
| 139 | 17/06/86 | Liane Aukin | Garth Tucker |
| 140 | 19/06/86 | Gerry Huxham | Garth Tucker |
| 141 | 24/06/86 | Susan Boyd | Matthew Robinson |
| 142 | 26/06/86 | Allan Swift | Matthew Robinson |
| 143 | 01/07/86 | Bill Lyons | Mike Gibbon |
| 144 | 03/07/86 | Rob Gittins | Mike Gibbon |
| 145 | 08/07/86 | Peter Batt | Garth Tucker |
| 146 | 10/07/86 | Tony McHale | Garth Tucker |
| 147 | 15/07/86 | Liane Aukin | William Slater |
| 148 | 17/07/86 | Gilly Fraser | William Slater |
| 149 | 22/07/86 | Gerry Huxham | M. Robinson/ Bren Simson |
| 150 | 24/07/86 | Jack Lewis | M. Robinson/ Bren Simson |
| 151 | 29/07/86 | Tony McHale | Alan Wareing |
| 152 | 31/07/86 | Peter Batt | Alan Wareing |
| 153 | 05/08/86 | Julia Schofield | William Slater |
| 154 | 07/08/86 | Bill Lyons | William Slater |
| 155 | 12/08/86 | Liane Aukin | Bren Simson |
| 156 | 14/08/86 | Tony Bilbow | Bren Simson |
| 157 | 19/08/86 | Rosemary Mason | Alan Wareing |
| 158 | 21/08/86 | Bev Doyle | Alan Wareing |
| 159 | 26/08/86 | Tony McHale | William Slater |
| 160 | 28/08/86 | Peter Batt | William Slater |
| 161 | 02/09/86 | Billy Hamon | Romey Allison |
| 162 | 04/09/86 | Bill Lyons | Romey Allison |
| 163 | 09/09/86 | Gilly Fraser | Alan Wareing |
| 164 | 11/09/86 | Jane Hollowood | Alan Wareing |
| 165 | 16/09/86 | Michael Robartes | Mike Lloyd |
| 166 | 18/09/86 | Bill Lyons | Mike Lloyd |
| 167 | 23/09/86 | Bill Lyons | Antonia Bird |
| 168 | 25/09/86 | David Ashton | Antonia Bird |
| 169 | 30/09/86 | Tony McHale | Mike Gibbon |
| 170 | 02/10/86 | Gerry Huxham | Mike Gibbon |
| 171 | 07/10/86 | Michael Robartes | Mike Lloyd |
| 172 | 09/10/86 | Bill Lyons | Mike Lloyd |
| 173 | 14/10/86 | Liane Aukin | Antonia Bird |
| 174 | 16/10/86 | Jane Hollowood | Antonia Bird |
| 175 | 21/10/86 | Gilly Fraser | Mike Gibbon |
| 176 | 23/10/86 | Bill Lyons | Mike Gibbon |
| 177 | 28/10/86 | Charlie Humphreys | Mike Lloyd |
| 178 | 30/10/86 | Michael Robartes | Mike Lloyd |
| 179 | 04/11/86 | Gilly Fraser | Antonia Bird |
| 180 | 06/11/86 | Tony McHale | Antonia Bird |
| 181 | 11/11/86 | Jane Hollowood | Mike Gibbon |
| 182 | 13/11/86 | Bill Lyons | Mike Gibbon |
| 183 | 18/11/86 | Tony Holland | Julia Smith |
| 184 | 20/11/86 | Tony Holland | Julia Smith |
| 185 | 25/11/86 | Tony Holland | Julia Smith |
| 186 | 27/11/86 | Gilly Fraser | Tony Virgo |
| 187 | 02/12/86 | Charlie Humphreys | Nick Prosser |

| Episode | Transmission date | Writer | Director |
|---|---|---|---|
| 188 | 04/12/86 | Michael Robartes | Nick Prosser |
| 189 | 09/12/86 | Liane Aukin | Garth Tucker |
| 190 | 11/12/86 | Gerry Huxham | Garth Tucker |
| 191 | 16/12/86 | Tony McHale | Tony Virgo |
| 192 | 18/12/86 | Billy Hamon | Tony Virgo |
| 193 | 23/12/86 | Bill Lyons | Nick Prosser |
| 194a | 25/12/86 | Tony Holland | Julia Smith |
| 194b | 25/12/86 | Tony Holland | Julia Smith |
| 195 | 30/12/86 | Gilly Fraser | Garth Tucker |
| 196 | 01/01/87 | Charlie Humphreys | Garth Tucker |
| 197 | 06/01/87 | Michael Robartes | Tony Virgo |
| 198 | 08/01/87 | Gerry Huxham | Tony Virgo |
| 199 | 13/01/87 | Bill Lyons | Nick Prosser |
| 200 | 15/01/87 | Juliet Ace | Nick Prosser |
| 201 | 20/01/87 | Tony McHale | Garth Tucker |
| 202 | 22/01/87 | Robin Allen | Garth Tucker |
| 203 | 27/01/87 | Michael Robartes | William Slater |
| 204 | 29/01/87 | Gerry Huxham | William Slater |
| 205 | 03/02/87 | Maureen Chadwick | Chris Clough |
| 206 | 05/02/87 | Charlie Humphreys | Chris Clough |
| 207 | 10/02/87 | Tony McHale | Romey Allison |
| 208 | 12/02/87 | Bill Lyons | Romey Allison |
| 209 | 17/02/87 | Jane Hollowood | William Slater |
| 210 | 19/02/87 | Mark Wheatley | William Slater |
| 211 | 24/02/87 | Rosemary Mason | Chris Clough |
| 212 | 26/02/87 | Charlie Humphreys | Chris Clough |
| 213 | 03/03/87 | Gilly Fraser | Romey Allison |
| 214 | 05/03/87 | Liane Aukin | Romey Allison |
| 215 | 10/03/87 | Michael Robartes | William Slater |
| 216 | 12/03/87 | Ayshe Raif | William Slater |
| 217 | 17/03/87 | Bill Lyons | Chris Clough |
| 218 | 19/03/87 | Jane Hollowood | Chris Clough |
| 219 | 24/03/87 | Rosemary Mason | Romey Allison |
| 220 | 26/03/87 | Charlie Humphreys | Romey Allison |
| 221 | 31/03/87 | Susan Boyd | Garth Tucker |
| 222 | 02/04/87 | Tony McHale | Garth Tucker |
| 223 | 07/04/87 | John Maynard | Tom Kingdom |
| 224 | 09/04/87 | Gilly Fraser | Tom Kingdom |
| 225 | 14/04/87 | Bill Lyons | Henry Foster |
| 226 | 16/04/87 | Tony McHale | Henry Foster |
| 227 | 21/04/87 | Bill Lyons | Garth Tucker |
| 228 | 23/04/87 | Bev Doyle | Garth Tucker |
| 229 | 28/04/87 | David Hopkins | Tom Kingdom |
| 230 | 30/04/87 | Rosemary Mason | Tom Kingdom |
| 231 | 05/05/87 | Tony McHale | Henry Foster |
| 232 | 07/05/87 | Bill Lyons | Tony Virgo |
| 233 | 12/05/87 | Gilly Fraser | Garth Tucker |
| 234 | 14/05/87 | Jane Hollowood | Garth Tucker |
| 235 | 19/05/87 | Charlie Humphreys | Tom Kingdom |
| 236 | 21/05/87 | Billy Hamon | Tom Kingdom |
| 237 | 26/05/87 | Rosemary Mason | Henry Foster |
| 238 | 28/05/87 | Gillian Richmond | Henry Foster |
| 239 | 02/06/87 | Gilly Fraser | Romey Allison |
| 240 | 04/06/87 | Liane Aukin | Romey Allison |
| 241 | 09/06/87 | Juliet Ace | Mike Gibbon |
| 242 | 11/06/87 | Sarah Daniels | Mike Gibbon |
| 243 | 16/06/87 | Michael Robartes | Nick Prosser |
| 244 | 18/06/87 | Rosemary Mason | Nick Prosser |
| 245 | 23/06/87 | Jane Hollowood | Henry Foster |
| 246 | 25/06/87 | Tony McHale | Henry Foster |
| 247 | 30/06/87 | Bill Lyons | Mike Gibbon |
| 248 | 02/07/87 | Charlie Humphreys | Mike Gibbon |
| 249 | 07/07/87 | Juliet Ace | Nick Prosser |
| 250 | 09/07/87 | Gilly Fraser | Nick Prosser |
| 251 | 14/07/87 | Michael Robartes | Romey Allison |
| 252 | 16/07/87 | Bill Lyons | Romey Allison |
| 253 | 21/07/87 | Jane Hollowood | Mike Gibbon |
| 254 | 23/07/87 | Tony McHale | Mike Gibbon |
| 255 | 28/07/87 | Gilly Fraser | Nick Prosser |
| 256 | 30/07/87 | Bill Lyons | Nick Prosser |
| 257 | 04/08/87 | Juliet Ace | Chris Lovett |
| 258 | 06/08/87 | Charlie Humphreys | Chris Lovett |
| 259 | 11/08/87 | Jane Hollowood | Henry Foster |
| 260 | 13/08/87 | Shirley Cooklin | Henry Foster |
| 261 | 18/08/87 | Tony McHale | Tom Kingdom |
| 262 | 20/08/87 | Michael Robartes | Tom Kingdom |
| 263 | 25/08/87 | Bill Lyons | Chris Lovett |
| 264 | 27/08/87 | Charlie Humphreys | Chris Lovett |
| 265 | 01/09/87 | Juliet Ace | Henry Foster |
| 266 | 03/09/87 | Gilly Fraser | Henry Foster |
| 267 | 08/09/87 | John Maynard | Tony Virgo |
| 268 | 10/09/87 | John Maynard | Tony Virgo |
| 269 | 15/09/87 | Carl Rigg | Tom Kingdom |
| 270 | 17/09/87 | Tony McHale | Tom Kingdom |
| 271 | 22/09/87 | Michael Robartes | Chris Lovett |
| 272 | 24/09/87 | Jane Hollowood | Chris Lovett |
| 273 | 29/09/87 | Bill Lyons | Henry Foster |
| 274 | 01/10/87 | Charlie Humphreys | Henry Foster |
| 275 | 06/10/87 | Mark Wheatley | Tom Kingdom |
| 276 | 08/10/87 | Rosemary Mason | Tom Kingdom |
| 277 | 13/10/87 | Jane Hollowood | Mervyn Cumming |
| 278 | 15/10/87 | Gilly Fraser | Mervyn Cumming |
| 279 | 20/10/87 | Tony Holland | Julia Smith |
| 280 | 22/10/87 | Tony Holland | Julia Smith |
| 281 | 27/10/87 | Michael Robartes | Garth Tucker |
| 282 | 29/10/87 | Tony McHale | Garth Tucker |
| 283 | 03/11/87 | Bill Lyons | Steve Goldie |
| 284 | 05/11/87 | Juliet Ace | Steve Goldie |
| 285 | 10/11/87 | Tony Holland | Mervyn Cumming |
| 286 | 12/11/87 | Charlie Humphreys | Mervyn Cumming |

| Episode | Transmission date | Writer | Director | Episode | Transmission date | Writer | Director |
|---|---|---|---|---|---|---|---|
| 287 | 17/11/87 | Gilly Fraser | Garth Tucker | 335 | 03/05/88 | Michael Robartes | Mervyn Cumming |
| 288 | 19/11/87 | Juliet Ace | Garth Tucker | 336 | 05/05/88 | Rosemary Mason | Mervyn Cumming |
| 289 | 24/11/87 | Jane Hollowood | Steve Goldie | 337 | 10/05/88 | Bill Lyons | Chris Lovett |
| 290 | 26/11/87 | Bill Lyons | Steve Goldie | 338 | 12/05/88 | Gilly Fraser | Chris Lovett |
| 291 | 01/12/87 | Bill Lyons | Mervyn Cumming | 339 | 17/05/88 | Juliet Ace | Jeremy Ancock |
| 292 | 03/12/87 | Tony McHale | Mervyn Cumming | 340 | 19/05/88 | Jane Hollowood | Jeremy Ancock |
| 293 | 08/12/87 | Liane Aukin | Garth Tucker | 341 | 24/05/88 | Jane Hollowood | Mervyn Cumming |
| 294 | 10/12/87 | Michael Robartes | Garth Tucker | 342 | 26/05/88 | Tony McHale | Mervyn Cumming |
| 295 | 15/12/87 | Michael Robartes | Steve Goldie | 343 | 31/05/88 | Susan Boyd | Chris Lovett |
| 296 | 17/12/87 | Gilly Fraser | Steve Goldie | 344 | 02/06/88 | Charlie Humphreys | Chris Lovett |
| 297 | 22/12/87 | Jane Hollowood | Tom Kingdom | 345 | 07/06/88 | Gilly Fraser | Jeremy Ancock |
| 298 | 24/12/87 | Charlie Humphreys | Tom Kingdom | 346 | 09/06/88 | Michael Robartes | Jeremy Ancock |
| 298a | 25/12/87 | Jane Hollowood | Matthew Robinson | 347 | 14/06/88 | Mark Wheatley | Mervyn Cumming |
| 299 | 29/12/87 | Bill Lyons | Julia Smith | 348 | 16/06/88 | Rob Gittins | Mervyn Cumming |
| 300 | 31/12/87 | Jane Hollowood | Julia Smith | 349 | 21/06/88 | Tony McHale | Chris Lovett |
| 300a | 31/12/87 | Jane Hollowood | Julia Smith | 350 | 23/06/88 | Gerry Huxham | Chris Lovett |
| 301 | 05/01/88 | Bill Lyons | William Slater | 351 | 28/06/88 | Juliet Ace | Jeremy Ancock |
| 302 | 07/01/88 | Liane Aukin | William Slater | 352 | 30/06/88 | Susan Boyd | Jeremy Ancock |
| 303 | 12/01/88 | Gilly Fraser | Tony Garrick | 353 | 05/07/88 | Gilly Fraser | Nick Prosser |
| 304 | 14/01/88 | Michael Robartes | Tony Garrick | 354 | 07/07/88 | Tony McHale | Nick Prosser |
| 305 | 19/01/88 | Charlie Humphreys | Tom Kingdom | 355 | 12/07/88 | Tony McHale | Garth Tucker |
| 306 | 21/01/88 | Tony McHale | Tom Kingdom | 356 | 14/07/88 | Tony McHale | Garth Tucker |
| 307 | 26/01/88 | Jane Hollowood | William Slater | 357 | 19/07/88 | Jane Hollowood | Nick Prosser |
| 308 | 28/01/88 | Bill Lyons | William Slater | 358 | 21/07/88 | Tony Holland | Julia Smith |
| 309 | 02/02/88 | Charlie Humphreys | Tom Kingdom | 358a | 26/07/88 | Tony Holland | Julia Smith |
| 310 | 04/02/88 | Liane Aukin | Tom Kingdom | 359 | 28/07/88 | Tony Holland | Julia Smith |
| 311 | 09/02/88 | Tony McHale | Tony Garrick | 360 | 02/08/88 | John Lewis | Nick Prosser |
| 312 | 11/02/88 | Rosemary Mason | Tony Garrick | 361 | 04/08/88 | Michael Robartes | Garth Tucker |
| 313 | 16/02/88 | Michael Robartes | William Slater | 362 | 09/08/88 | Jane Hollowood | Garth Tucker |
| 314 | 18/02/88 | Gilly Fraser | William Slater | 363 | 11/08/88 | Gerry Huxham | Tony Garrick |
| 315 | 23/02/88 | Charlie Humphreys | Tony Virgo | 364 | 16/08/88 | Bill Lyons | Tony Garrick |
| 316 | 25/02/88 | Tony McHale | Tony Virgo | 365 | 18/08/88 | Liane Aukin | Nick Prosser |
| 317 | 01/03/88 | Tony McHale | Chris Clough | 366 | 23/08/88 | Tony McHale | Nick Prosser |
| 318 | 03/03/88 | Bill Lyons | Chris Clough | 367 | 25/08/88 | Tony Holland | Garth Tucker |
| 319 | 08/03/88 | Gilly Fraser | Peter Edwards | 368 | 30/08/88 | John Drew | Garth Tucker |
| 320 | 10/03/88 | Jane Hollowood | Peter Edwards | 369 | 01/09/88 | Susan Boyd | Philip Draycott |
| 321 | 15/03/88 | Rosemary Mason | Steve Goldie | 370 | 06/09/88 | Charlie Humphreys | Philip Draycott |
| 322 | 15/03/88 | Michael Robartes | Steve Goldie | 371 | 08/09/88 | Bill Lyons | Peter Edwards |
| 323 | 22/03/88 | Charlie Humphreys | Chris Clough | 372 | 13/09/88 | Bill Lyons | Peter Edwards |
| 324 | 24/03/88 | John Maynard | Chris Clough | 372a | 15/09/88 | John Maynard | Julia Smith |
| 325 | 29/03/88 | Liane Aukin | Peter Edwards | 373 | 20/09/88 | Jane Galletly | William Slater |
| 326 | 31/03/88 | Gillian Richmond | Peter Edwards | 374 | 22/09/88 | Charlie Humphreys | William Slater |
| 327 | 05/04/88 | Rosemary Mason | Steve Goldie | 375 | 27/09/88 | Susan Boyd | Frank Cox |
| 328 | 07/04/88 | Michael Robartes | Steve Goldie | 376 | 29/09/88 | Jane Hollowood | Frank Cox |
| 329 | 12/04/88 | Juliet Ace | Chris Clough | 377 | 04/10/88 | Bill Lyons | Steve Goldie |
| 330 | 14/04/88 | Tony McHale | Chris Clough | 378 | 06/10/88 | Tony Holland | Steve Goldie |
| 331 | 19/04/88 | Tony McHale | Peter Edwards | 379 | 11/10/88 | Gilly Fraser | William Slater |
| 332 | 21/04/88 | Gilly Fraser | Peter Edwards | 380 | 13/10/88 | Rob Gittins | William Slater |
| 333 | 26/04/88 | Susan Boyd | Steve Goldie | 381 | 18/10/88 | Charlie Humphreys | Frank Cox |
| 334 | 28/04/88 | Charlie Humphreys | Steve Goldie | 382 | 20/10/88 | Jane Hollowood | Frank Cox |

| Episode | Transmission date | Writer | Director | Episode | Transmission date | Writer | Director |
|---|---|---|---|---|---|---|---|
| 383 | 25/10/88 | Michael Robartes | Steve Goldie | 433 | 18/04/89 | Gilly Fraser | Philip Draycott |
| 384 | 27/10/88 | David Ashton | Steve Goldie | 434 | 20/04/89 | Ayshe Raif | Philip Draycott |
| 385 | 01/11/88 | Gilly Fraser | William Slater | 435 | 25/04/89 | Michael Robartes | Gerald Blake |
| 386 | 03/11/88 | Gerry Huxham | William Slater | 436 | 27/04/89 | Jane Hollowood | Chris Lovett |
| 387 | 08/11/88 | Bill Lyons | Frank Cox | 437 | 02/05/89 | Jane Hollowood | Chris Lovett |
| 388 | 10/11/88 | Mark Thomas | Frank Cox | 438 | 04/05/89 | Gerry Huxham | Gerald Blake |
| 389 | 15/11/88 | John Drew | Steve Goldie | 439 | 09/05/89 | Rob Gittins | Garth Tucker |
| 390 | 17/11/88 | Charlie Humphreys | Steve Goldie | 440 | 11/05/89 | John Maynard | Garth Tucker |
| 391 | 22/11/88 | Michael Robartes | Jeremy Silberston | 441 | 16/05/89 | Tony McHale | Philip Draycott |
| 392 | 24/11/88 | Jane Hollowood | Jeremy Silberston | 442 | 18/05/89 | Tony McHale | Philip Draycott |
| 393 | 29/11/88 | Gilly Fraser | Mervyn Cumming | 443 | 23/05/89 | Gilly Fraser | Gerald Blake |
| 394 | 01/12/88 | Rob Gittins | Mervyn Cumming | 444 | 25/05/89 | Tony Jordan | Gerald Blake |
| 395 | 06/12/88 | Gerry Huxham | Philip Draycott | 445 | 30/05/89 | Susan Boyd | Chris Lovett |
| 396 | 08/12/88 | Gillian Richmond | Philip Draycott | 446 | 01/06/89 | Tony McHale | Chris Lovett |
| 397 | 13/12/88 | Liane Aukin | Philip Draycott | 447 | 06/06/89 | Gillian Richmond | Garth Tucker |
| 398 | 15/12/88 | Bill Lyons | Philip Draycott | 448 | 08/06/89 | Ayshe Raif | Garth Tucker |
| 399 | 20/12/88 | Juliet Ace | Mervyn Cumming | 449 | 13/06/89 | Bill Lyons | Philip Draycott |
| 400 | 22/12/88 | Tony Holland | Julia Smith | 450 | 15/06/89 | Rob Gittins | Philip Draycott |
| 401 | 27/12/88 | Charlie Humphreys | Jeremy Silberston | 451 | 20/06/89 | Tony McHale | Chris Lovett |
| 402 | 29/12/88 | Michael Robartes | Jeremy Silberston | 452 | 22/06/89 | Tony Jordan | Chris Lovett |
| 403 | 03/01/89 | John Maynard | Jeremy Silberston | 453 | 27/06/89 | Tony McHale | Gerald Blake |
| 404 | 05/01/89 | Tony Holland | Julia Smith | 454 | 29/06/89 | Charlie Humphreys | Gerald Blake |
| 405 | 10/01/89 | Jane Galletly | Mervyn Cumming | 455 | 04/07/89 | Jane Hollowood | Garth Tucker |
| 406 | 12/01/89 | Mark Wheatley | Mervyn Cumming | 456 | 06/07/89 | Michael Robartes | Garth Tucker |
| 407 | 17/01/89 | Tony McHale | Philip Draycott | 457 | 11/07/89 | Gerry Huxham | Philip Draycott |
| 408 | 19/01/89 | Bill Lyons | Philip Draycott | 458 | 13/07/89 | Juliet Ace | Philip Draycott |
| 409 | 24/01/89 | Gillian Richmond | William Slater | 459 | 18/07/89 | Juliet Ace | Gerald Blake |
| 410 | 26/01/89 | Gilly Fraser | William Slater | 460 | 20/07/89 | Gilly Fraser | Gerald Blake |
| 411 | 31/01/89 | Juliet Ace | Steve Goldie | 461 | 25/07/89 | Graeme Curry | William Slater |
| 412 | 02/02/89 | Jane Hollowood | Steve Goldie | 462 | 27/07/89 | Charlie Humphreys | William Slater |
| 413 | 07/02/89 | Charlie Humphreys | Terry Iland | 463 | 01/08/89 | Tony McHale | Darrol Blake |
| 414 | 09/02/89 | Tony McHale | Terry Iland | 464 | 03/08/89 | Tony McHale | Darrol Blake |
| 415 | 14/02/89 | Tony Holland | William Slater | 465 | 08/08/89 | Jane Hollowood | Robert Gabriel |
| 416 | 16/02/89 | Bill Lyons | William Slater | 466 | 10/08/89 | Jane Hollowood | Robert Gabriel |
| 417 | 21/02/89 | Bill Lyons | Julia Smith | 467 | 15/08/89 | Tony Jordan | Mervyn Cumming |
| 418 | 23/02/89 | John Lewis | Julia Smith | 468 | 17/08/89 | Michael Robartes | Mervyn Cumming |
| 419 | 28/02/89 | Michael Robartes | Steve Goldie | 469 | 22/08/89 | Susan Boyd | William Slater |
| 420 | 02/03/89 | Rosemary Mason | Steve Goldie | 470 | 24/08/89 | Rob Gittins | William Slater |
| 421 | 07/03/89 | Charlie Humphreys | Terry Iland | 471 | 29/08/89 | Tony Jordan | Darrol Blake |
| 422 | 09/03/89 | Rob Gittins | Terry Iland | 472 | 31/08/89 | Tony Jordan | Darrol Blake |
| 423 | 14/03/89 | Gilly Fraser | William Slater | 473 | 05/09/89 | Gilly Fraser | Robert Gabriel |
| 424 | 16/03/89 | Gilly Fraser | William Slater | 474 | 07/09/89 | Gilly Fraser | Robert Gabriel |
| 425 | 21/03/89 | Susan Boyd | Steve Goldie | 475 | 12/09/89 | Tony McHale | Mervyn Cumming |
| 426 | 23/03/89 | Juliet Ace | Steve Goldie | 476 | 14/09/89 | Tony McHale | Mervyn Cumming |
| 427 | 28/03/89 | Juliet Ace | Mervyn Cumming | 477 | 19/09/89 | Charlie Humphreys | William Slater |
| 428 | 30/03/89 | Allan Swift | Mervyn Cumming | 478 | 21/09/89 | Charlie Humphreys | William Slater |
| 429 | 04/04/89 | Tony McHale | Mike Gibbon | 479 | 26/09/89 | Juliet Ace | Darrol Blake |
| 430 | 06/04/89 | Tony Jordan | Chris Lovett | 480 | 28/09/89 | Graeme Curry | Darrol Blake |
| 431 | 11/04/89 | Charlie Humphreys | Garth Tucker | 481 | 03/10/89 | Gillian Richmond | Peter Boisseau |
| 432 | 13/04/89 | Charlie Humphreys | Garth Tucker | 482 | 05/10/89 | John Maynard | Peter Boisseau |

| Episode | Transmission date | Writer | Director | Episode | Transmission date | Writer | Director |
|---|---|---|---|---|---|---|---|
| 483 | 10/10/89 | Tony McHale | Mervyn Cumming | 533 | 03/04/90 | Tony McHale | Michael Kerrigan |
| 484 | 12/10/89 | Tony Jordan | Mervyn Cumming | 534 | 05/04/90 | Tony McHale | Michael Kerrigan |
| 485 | 17/10/89 | Michael Robartes | William Slater | 535 | 10/04/90 | Brendan Cassin | Matthew Evans |
| 486 | 19/10/89 | Charlie Humphreys | William Slater | 536 | 12/04/90 | Brendan Cassin | Matthew Evans |
| 487 | 24/10/89 | Liane Aukin | Darrol Blake | 537 | 17/04/90 | Gillian Richmond | Chris Hodson |
| 488 | 26/10/89 | John Crisp | Darrol Blake | 538 | 19/04/90 | Gillian Richmond | Chris Hodson |
| 489 | 31/10/89 | Tony Jordan | Peter Boisseau | 539 | 24/04/90 | John Maynard | Philip Casson |
| 490 | 02/11/89 | Jane Galletly | Peter Boisseau | 540 | 26/04/90 | John Maynard | Philip Casson |
| 491 | 07/11/89 | Charlie Humphreys | Mervyn Cumming | 541 | 01/05/90 | Tony Jordan | Michael Kerrigan |
| 492 | 09/11/89 | Sarah Daniels | Mervyn Cumming | 542 | 03/05/90 | Tony Jordan | Michael Kerrigan |
| 493 | 14/11/89 | Juliet Ace | Darrol Blake | 543 | 08/05/90 | Michael Russell | Matthew Evans |
| 494 | 16/11/89 | Tony McHale | Darrol Blake | 544 | 10/05/90 | Michael Russell | Matthews Evans |
| 495 | 21/11/89 | Susan Boyd | Philip Draycott | 545 | 15/05/90 | Tony McHale | Leonard Lewis |
| 496 | 23/11/89 | Gary Hopkins | Philip Draycott | 546 | 17/05/90 | Tony McHale | Leonard Lewis |
| 497 | 28/11/89 | Ayshe Raif | Mervyn Cumming | 547 | 22/05/90 | Peter Hammond | David Crozier |
| 498 | 30/11/89 | Tony Jordan | Mervyn Cumming | 548 | 24/05/90 | Peter Hammond | David Crozier |
| 499 | 05/12/89 | Tony McHale | Matthew Evans | 549 | 29/05/90 | Paul Doust | Barry Letts |
| 500 | 07/12/89 | Tony McHale | Matthew Evans | 550 | 31/05/90 | Paul Doust | Barry Letts |
| 501 | 12/12/89 | Charlie Humphreys | Nick Prosser | 551 | 05/06/90 | Ayshe Raif | Mervyn Cumming |
| 502 | 14/12/89 | Charlie Humphreys | Nick Prosser | 552 | 07/06/90 | Gerry Huxham | Mervyn Cumming |
| 503 | 19/12/89 | Jane Galletly | Darrol Blake | 553 | 12/06/90 | John Maynard | Leonard Lewis |
| 504 | 21/12/89 | Paul Doust | Darrol Blake | 554 | 14/06/90 | John Maynard | Leonard Lewis |
| 505 | 26/12/89 | Tony McHale | Philip Draycott | 555 | 19/06/90 | Linda Dearsley/ Steve Waye | David Crozier |
| 506 | 28/12/89 | Sarah Daniels | Philip Draycott | | | | |
| 507 | 02/01/90 | Rob Gittins | Mervyn Cumming | 556 | 21/06/90 | Linda Dearsley/ Steve Waye | David Crozier |
| 508 | 04/01/90 | Tony McHale | Mervyn Cumming | | | | |
| 509 | 09/01/90 | Tony Grounds | Matthew Evans | 557 | 26/06/90 | Deborah Cook | Barry Letts |
| 510 | 11/01/90 | Ayshe Raif | Matthew Evans | 558 | 28/06/90 | Deborah Cook | Barry Letts |
| 511 | 16/01/90 | Tony Jordan | Darrol Blake | 559 | 03/07/90 | Tony McHale | Michael Ferguson |
| 512 | 18/01/90 | Tony Jordan | Darrol Blake | 560 | 05/07/90 | Michael Ellis | Michael Ferguson |
| 513 | 23/01/90 | Gilly Fraser | Philip Draycott | 561 | 10/07/90 | Christopher Penfold | Mervyn Cumming |
| 514 | 25/01/90 | Gilly Fraser | Philip Draycott | 562 | 12/07/90 | John Milne | Mervyn Cumming |
| 515 | 30/01/90 | Tony McHale | Mervyn Cumming | 563 | 17/07/90 | Tony Jordan | Matthew Evans |
| 516 | 01/02/90 | Tony McHale | Mervyn Cumming | 564 | 19/07/90 | Tony Jordan | Matthew Evans |
| 517 | 06/02/90 | John Maynard | Sheila Atha | 565 | 24/07/90 | Gerry Huxham | Barry Letts |
| 518 | 08/02/90 | Gillian Richmond | Sheila Atha | 566 | 26/07/90 | Rob Gittins | Bary Letts |
| 519 | 13/02/90 | Tony Jordan | Darrol Blake | 567 | 31/07/90 | Michael Russell | Alister Hallum |
| 520 | 15/02/90 | Rob Gittins | Darrol Blake | 568 | 02/08/90 | Robin Mukherjee | Alister Hallum |
| 521 | 20/02/90 | Tony McHale | Philip Draycott | 569 | 07/08/90 | Juliet Ace | Mervyn Cumming |
| 522 | 22/02/90 | Tony McHale | Philip Draycott | 570 | 09/08/90 | Liane Aukin | Mervyn Cumming |
| 523 | 27/02/90 | Tony Grounds | Mervyn Cumming | 571 | 14/08/90 | Brendan Cassin | Matthew Evans |
| 524 | 01/03/90 | Juliet Ace | Mervyn Cumming | 572 | 16/08/90 | Gillian Richmond | Matthew Evans |
| 525 | 06/03/90 | Paul Doust | Sheila Atha | 573 | 21/08/90 | Tony McHale | Barry Letts |
| 526 | 08/03/90 | Rosemary Mason | Sheila Atha | 574 | 23/08/90 | Tony McHale | Barry Letts |
| 527 | 13/03/90 | Tony Jordan | Chris Hodson | 575 | 28/08/90 | Charlie Humphreys | Alister Hallum |
| 528 | 15/03/90 | Tony Jordan | Chris Hodson | 576 | 30/08/90 | Charlie Humphreys | Alister Hallum |
| 529 | 20/03/90 | Debbie Cook | Philip Casson | 577 | 04/09/90 | Tony Jordan | Paul Harrison |
| 530 | 22/03/90 | Debbie Cook | Philip Casson | 578 | 06/09/90 | Tony Jordan | Paul Harrison |
| 531 | 27/03/90 | Tony McHale | Mike Barnes | 579 | 11/09/90 | Debbie Cook | Matthew Evans |
| 532 | 29/03/90 | Tony McHale | Mike Barnes | 580 | 13/09/90 | Debbie Cook | Matthew Evans |

| Episode | Transmission date | Writer | Director |
|---|---|---|---|
| 581 | 18/09/90 | Chris Penfold | Barry Letts |
| 582 | 20/09/90 | Gerry Huxham | Barry Letts |
| 583 | 25/09/90 | Susan Boyd | Nick Prosser |
| 584 | 27/09/90 | Jez Simons/Jyoti Patel | Nick Prosser |
| 585 | 01/10/90 | Linda Dearsley/ Steve Waye | Paul Harrison |
| 586 | 04/10/90 | Linda Dearsley/ Steve Waye | Paul Harrison |
| 587 | 09/10/90 | Sarah Daniels | Mervyn Cumming |
| 588 | 11/10/90 | Winsome Pinnock | Mervyn Cumming |
| 589 | 16/10/90 | Paul Doust | Charles Beeson |
| 590 | 18/10/90 | Paul Doust | Charles Beeson |
| 591 | 23/10/90 | Charlie Humphreys | Nick Prosser |
| 592 | 25/10/90 | Charlie Humphreys | Nick Prosser |
| 593 | 30/10/90 | Michael Russell | Leonard Lewis |
| 594 | 01/11/90 | John Milne | Leonard Lewis |
| 595 | 06/11/90 | Debbie Cook | Mike Barnes |
| 596 | 08/11/90 | Debbie Cook | Mike Barnes |
| 597 | 13/11/90 | Tony McHale | Michael Ferguson |
| 598 | 15/11/90 | Tony McHale | Michael Ferguson |
| 599 | 20/11/90 | Chris Penfold | Barry Letts |
| 600 | 22/11/90 | Gerry Huxham | Barry Letts |
| 601 | 27/11/90 | Gillian Richmond | Philip Casson |
| 602 | 29/11/90 | Sean Egan | Philip Casson |
| 603 | 04/12/90 | Rob Gittins | Leonard Lewis |
| 604 | 06/12/90 | Matthew Holt | Leonard Lewis |
| 605 | 11/12/90 | Tony Jordan | Philip Casson |
| 606 | 13/12/90 | Tony Jordan | Philip Casson |
| 607 | 18/12/90 | John Milne | Paul Bernard |
| 608 | 20/12/90 | John Milne | Paul Bernard |
| 609 | 25/12/90 | Michael Russell | Alan Wareing |
| 610 | 27/12/90 | Michael Russell | Alan Wareing |
| 611 | 01/01/91 | Linda Dearsley/ Steve Waye | Charles Beeson |
| 612 | 03/01/91 | Ayshe Raif | Charles Beeson |
| 613 | 08/01/91 | Tony McHale | Richard Holthouse |
| 614 | 10/01/91 | Tony McHale | Richard Holthouse |
| 615 | 15/01/91 | Gerry Huxham | Stephen Butcher |
| 616 | 17/01/91 | Gerry Huxham | Stephen Butcher |
| 617 | 22/01/91 | Michael Ellis | Nick Prosser |
| 618 | 24/01/91 | Deborah Cook | Nick Prosser |
| 619 | 29/01/91 | Tony Jordan | Charles Beeson |
| 620 | 31/01/91 | Tony Jordan | Charles Beeson |
| 621 | 07/02/91 | Charlie Humphreys | Terry Iland |
| 622 | 09/02/91 | Charlie Humphreys | Terry Iland |
| 623 | 12/02/91 | Rob Gittins | Stephen Butcher |
| 624 | 14/02/91 | Margaret Simpson | Stephen Butcher |
| 625 | 19/02/91 | Charlie Humphreys | Nick Prosser |
| 626 | 21/02/91 | Susan Boyd | Nick Prosser |
| 627 | 26/02/91 | Tony McHale | Charles Beeson |
| 628 | 28/02/91 | Tony McHale | Charles Beeson |
| 629 | 03/03/91 | Jyoti Patel/Jez Simons | Terry Iland |
| 630 | 07/03/91 | Trish Cooke | Terry Iland |
| 631 | 12/03/91 | Chris Penfold | Jonathan Wright Miller |
| 632 | 14/03/91 | Linda Dearsley/ Steve Waye | Jonathan Wright Miller |
| 633 | 19/03/91 | Tony Jordan | Mervyn Cumming |
| 634 | 21/03/91 | Tony Jordan | Mervyn Cumming |
| 635 | 26/03/91 | John Milne | Charles Beeson |
| 636 | 28/03/91 | Gerry Huxham | Charles Beeson |
| 637 | 02/04/91 | Lisa Evans | Jean Stewert |
| 638 | 04/04/91 | Sean Egan | Jean Stewert |
| 639 | 09/04/91 | Rob Gittins | Jonathan Wright Miller |
| 640 | 11/04/91 | Tony Jordan | Jonathan Wright Miller |
| 641 | 16/04/91 | Tony McHale | Mervyn Cumming |
| 642 | 18/04/91 | Tony McHale | Mervyn Cumming |
| 643 | 23/04/91 | Linda Dearsley/ Steve Waye | Barry Letts |
| 644 | 25/04/91 | Barrie Shore | Barry Letts |
| 645 | 30/04/91 | Debbie Cook | Jean Stewert |
| 646 | 02/05/91 | Debbie Cook | Jean Stewert |
| 647 | 07/05/91 | Tony Jordan | Leonard Lewis |
| 648 | 09/05/91 | Tony Jordan | Leonard Lewis |
| 649 | 14/05/91 | Michael Russell | Philip Casson |
| 650 | 16/05/91 | Michael Russell | Philip Casson |
| 651 | 21/05/91 | Gerry Huxham | Douglas Argent |
| 652 | 23/05/91 | Jez Simons/Jyoti Patel | Douglas Argent |
| 653 | 28/05/91 | Brendan Cassin | Geoff Feld |
| 654 | 30/05/91 | Ashley Pharoah | Geoff Feld |
| 655 | 04/06/91 | Charlie Humphreys | Leonard Lewis |
| 656 | 06/06/91 | Charlie Humphreys | Leonard Lewis |
| 657 | 11/06/91 | Tony McHale | Philip Casson |
| 658 | 13/06/91 | Gillian Richmond | Philip Casson |
| 659 | 18/06/91 | Tony McHale | Charles Beeson |
| 660 | 20/06/91 | Tony McHale | Charles Beeson |
| 661 | 25/06/91 | Helen Millar | Richard Holthouse |
| 662 | 27/06/91 | Lisa Evans | Richard Holthouse |
| 663 | 02/07/91 | Debbie Cook | Terry Iland |
| 664 | 04/07/91 | Debbie Cook | Terry Iland |
| 665 | 09/07/91 | Rob Gittins | Mike Dormer |
| 666 | 11/07/91 | Linda Dearsley/ Steve Waye | Mike Dormer |
| 667 | 16/07/91 | Tony Jordan | Philip Casson |
| 668 | 18/07/91 | Tony Jordan | Philip Casson |
| 669 | 23/07/91 | Grazyna Monvid | David Andrews |
| 670 | 25/07/91 | Barrie Shore | David Andrews |
| 671 | 30/07/91 | Jyoti Patel/Jez Simons | Richard Holthouse |

| Episode | Transmission date | Writer | Director | Episode | Transmission date | Writer | Director |
|---------|-------------------|--------|----------|---------|-------------------|--------|----------|
| 672 | 01/08/91 | Gerry Huxham | Richard Holthouse | 717 | 07/01/92 | Tony Jordan | Philip Casson |
| 673 | 06/08/91 | Charlie Humphreys | Mike Dormer | 718 | 09/01/92 | Tony Jordan | Philip Casson |
| 674 | 08/08/91 | Charlie Humphreys | Mike Dormer | 719 | 14/01/92 | S. Stratford/A. Forbes | Jonathan Wright Miller |
| 675 | 13/08/91 | Brendan Cassin | Philip Casson | | | | |
| 676 | 15/08/91 | Brendan Cassin | Philip Casson | 720 | 16/01/92 | Barrie Shore | Jonathan Wright Miller |
| 677 | 20/08/91 | Lesley Davies | John Bruce | | | | |
| 678 | 22/08/91 | Michael Russell | John Bruce | 721 | 21/01/92 | Charlie Humphreys | David Innes Edwards |
| 679 | 27/08/91 | Ashley Pharoah | Jean Stewart | | | | |
| 680 | 29/08/91 | Andrew Holden | Jean Stewart | 722 | 23/01/92 | Charlie Humphreys | David Innes Edwards |
| 681 | 03/09/91 | Deborah Cook | Bill Hays | | | | |
| 682 | 05/09/91 | Deborah Cook | Bill Hays | 723 | 28/01/92 | John Chambers | Charles Beeson |
| 683 | 10/09/91 | Tony McHale | Geoff Feld | 724 | 30/01/92 | Susan Boyd | Charles Beeson |
| 684 | 12/09/91 | Tony McHale | Geoff Feld | 725 | 04/02/92 | Jez Simons/Jyoti Patel | Philip Casson |
| 685 | 17/09/91 | Tony Jordan | John Bruce | 726 | 06/02/92 | Helen Millar | Philip Casson |
| 686 | 19/09/91 | Tony Jordan | John Bruce | 727 | 11/02/92 | Deborah Cook | Mike Dormer |
| 687 | 24/09/91 | Sue Boyd | Jean Stewart | 728 | 13/02/92 | Deborah Cook | Mike Dormer |
| 688 | 26/09/91 | Lisa Evans | Jean Stewart | 729 | 18/02/92 | Ashley Pharoah | Nick Prosser |
| 689 | 01/10/91 | Gillian Richmond | Bill Hays | 730 | 20/02/92 | Ashley Pharoah | Nick Prosser |
| 690 | 03/10/91 | Barrie Shore | Bill Hays | 731 | 25/02/92 | Tony McHale | Barry Letts |
| 691 | 08/10/91 | Michael Russell | Geoff Feld | 732 | 27/02/92 | Tony McHale | Barry Letts |
| 692 | 10/10/91 | Michael Russell | Geoff Feld | 733 | 03/03/92 | Tony McHale | Geoff Feld |
| 693 | 15/10/91 | Lesley Davies | Barry Letts | 734 | 05/03/92 | Tony McHale | Geoff Feld |
| 694 | 17/10/91 | Gerry Huxham | Barry Letts | 735 | 10/03/92 | Judy Forshaw | Bill Hays |
| 695 | 22/10/91 | Ashley Pharoah | Philip Casson | 736 | 12/03/92 | Brendan Cassin | Bill Hays |
| 696 | 24/10/91 | Ashley Pharoah | Philip Casson | 737 | 17/03/92 | Lisa Evans | Matthew Evans |
| 697 | 29/10/91 | Tony McHale | Sue Dunderdale | 738 | 19/03/92 | Barrie Shore | Matthew Evans |
| 698 | 31/10/91 | Tony McHale | Sue Dunderdale | 739 | 24/03/92 | Tony Jordan | Barry Letts |
| 699 | 05/11/91 | Jyoti Patel/Jez Simons | Richard Holthouse | 740 | 26/03/92 | Tony Jordan | Barry Letts |
| 700 | 07/11/91 | Rosemary Mason | Richard Holthouse | 741 | 31/03/92 | Sue Boyd | Geoff Feld |
| 701 | 12/11/91 | Tony Jordan | Mike Dormer | 742 | 02/04/92 | Sue Boyd | Geoff Feld |
| 702 | 14/11/91 | Tony Jordan | Mike Dormer | 743 | 07/04/92 | Charlie Humphreys | Jonathan Wright Miller |
| 703 | 19/11/91 | Susan Boyd | Barry Letts | | | | |
| 704 | 21/11/91 | Linda Dearsley/ Steve Waye | Barry Letts | 744 | 09/04/92 | Charlie Humphreys | Jonathan Wright Miller |
| 705 | 26/11/91 | Brendan Cassin | Jean Stewart | 745 | 14/04/92 | Helen Millar | Beryl Richards |
| 706 | 28/11/91 | Brendan Cassin | Jean Stewart | 746 | 16/04/92 | Michael Robartes | Beryl Richards |
| 707 | 03/12/91 | Gerry Huxham | Douglas Argent | 747 | 21/04/92 | Tony Jordan | John Bruce |
| 708 | 05/12/91 | Gerry Huxham | Douglas Argent | 748 | 23/04/92 | Arnold Yarrow | John Bruce |
| 709 | 10/12/91 | Lisa Evans | Richard Holthouse | 749 | 28/04/92 | Barrie Shore | David Innes Edwards |
| 710 | 12/12/91 | Judy Forshaw | Richard Holthouse | | | | |
| 711 | 17/12/91 | Michael Russell | Jonathan Wright Miller | 750 | 30/04/92 | Lisa Evans | David Innes Edwards |
| 712 | 19/12/91 | Michael Russell | Jonathan Wright Miller | 751 | 05/05/92 | Debbie Cook | Jonathan Wright Miller |
| 713 | 24/12/91 | Tony McHale | David Innes Edwards | 752 | 07/05/92 | Debbie Cook | Jonathan Wright Miller |
| 714 | 26/12/91 | Tony McHale | David Innes Edwards | 753 | 12/05/92 | Gillian Richmond | Beryl Richards |
| | | | | 754 | 14/05/92 | Gillian Richmond | Beryl Richards |
| 715 | 31/12/91 | Debbie Cook | Charles Beeson | 755 | 19/05/92 | Tony Jordan | Sue Dunderdale |
| 716 | 02/01/92 | Debbie Cook | Charles Beeson | 756 | 21/05/92 | Tony Jordan | Sue Dunderdale |

| Episode | Transmission date | Writer | Director | Episode | Transmission date | Writer | Director |
|---|---|---|---|---|---|---|---|
| 757 | 26/05/92 | Susan Boyd | Mike Dormer | 805 | 10/11/92 | Tony McHale | Tony McHale |
| 758 | 28/05/92 | Susan Boyd | Mike Dormer | 806 | 12/11/92 | Tony McHale | Tony McHale |
| 759 | 02/06/92 | Arnold Yarrow | Bill Hays | 807 | 17/11/92 | Matthew Graham | Indra Bhose |
| 760 | 04/06/92 | Michael Robartes | Bill Hays | 808 | 19/11/92 | Jeff Povey | Indra Bhose |
| 761 | 09/06/92 | Tony McHale | Roger Gartland | 809 | 24/11/92 | Barrie Shore | Terry Iland |
| 762 | 11/06/92 | Tony McHale | Roger Gartland | 810 | 26/11/92 | Barrie Shore | Terry Iland |
| 763 | 16/06/92 | Brendan Cassin | Charles Beeson | 811 | 01/12/92 | Tony Jordan | Bill Hays |
| 764 | 18/06/92 | Brendan Cassin | Charles Beeson | 812 | 03/12/92 | Tony Jordan | Bill Hays |
| 765 | 23/06/92 | Debbie Cook | Leonard Lewis | 813 | 08/12/92 | Lilie Ferrari | Mike Dormer |
| 766 | 25/06/92 | Debbie Cook | Leonard Lewis | 814 | 10/12/92 | Duncan Gould | Mike Dormer |
| 767 | 30/06/92 | Ashley Pharoah | Philip Casson | 815 | 15/12/92 | Matthew Graham | Simon Meyers |
| 768 | 02/07/92 | Ashley Pharoah | Philip Casson | 816 | 17/12/92 | Michael Robartes | Simon Meyers |
| 769 | 07/07/92 | Lilie Ferrari | Bill Hays | 817 | 22/12/92 | Tony McHale | Roger Gartland |
| 770 | 09/07/92 | Michael Robartes | Bill Hays | 818 | 24/12/92 | Tony McHale | Roger Gartland |
| 771 | 14/07/92 | Barrie Shore | Roger Gartland | 818a | 25/12/92 | Tony McHale | Leonard Lewis |
| 772 | 16/07/92 | Arnold Yarrow | Roger Gartland | 819 | 29/12/92 | Kolton Lee | Bill Hays |
| 773 | 21/07/92 | Tony Jordan | Beryl Richards | 820 | 31/12/92 | Colin Brake | Bill Hays |
| 774 | 23/07/92 | Tony Jordan | Beryl Richards | 821 | 05/01/93 | Jeff Povey | Gwennan Sage |
| 775 | 28/07/92 | Susan Boyd | Philip Casson | 822 | 07/01/93 | Arnold Yarrow | Gwennan Sage |
| 776 | 30/07/92 | Susan Boyd | Philip Casson | 823 | 12/01/93 | Jonathan Myerson | Roger Gartland |
| 777 | 04/08/92 | Tony McHale | Paul Unwin | 824 | 14/01/93 | Tony Jordan | Roger Gartland |
| 778 | 06/08/92 | Tony McHale | Paul Unwin | 825 | 19/01/93 | Tony Jordan | Paul Unwin |
| 779 | 11/08/92 | Matthew Graham | Ronnie Wilson | 826 | 21/01/93 | Tony Jordan | Paul Unwin |
| 780 | 13/08/92 | Ashley Pharoah | Ronnie Wilson | 827 | 26/01/93 | Ashley Pharoah | Jonathan Wright Miller |
| 781 | 18/08/92 | Ashley Pharoah | Margy Kinmonth | 828 | 28/01/93 | Ashley Pharoah | Jonathan Wright Miller |
| 782 | 20/08/92 | Ashley Pharoah | Margy Kinmouth | 829 | 02/02/93 | Gillian Richmond | Sue Dunderdale |
| 783 | 25/08/92 | Michael Robartes | Bill Hays | 830 | 04/02/93 | Gillian Richmond | Sue Dunderdale |
| 784 | 27/08/92 | Tony McHale | Bill Hays | 831 | 09/02/93 | Duncan Gould | Bill Hays |
| 785 | 01/09/92 | Tony Jordan | Sue Dunderdale | 832 | 11/02/93 | Ashley Pharoah | Bill Hays |
| 786 | 03/09/92 | Tony Jordan | Sue Dunderdale | 833 | 16/02/93 | Kolton Lee | Geoff Feld |
| 787 | 08/09/92 | Barrie Shore | Ronnie Wilson | 834 | 18/02/93 | Lilie Ferrari | Geoff Feld |
| 788 | 10/09/92 | Barrie Shore | Ronnie Wilson | 835 | 23/02/93 | Matthew Graham | Jonathan Wright Miller |
| 789 | 15/09/92 | Gillian Richmond | Margy Kinmonth | 836 | 25/02/93 | Matthew Graham | Jonathan Wright Miller |
| 790 | 17/09/92 | Gillian Richmond | Margy Kinmonth | 837 | 02/03/93 | Tony Jordan | Sue Dunderdale |
| 791 | 22/09/92 | Deborah Cook | Jonathan Wright Miller | 838 | 04/03/93 | Tony Jordan | Sue Dunderdale |
| 792 | 24/09/92 | Deborah Cook | Jonathan Wright Miller | 839 | 09/03/93 | Susan Boyd | Philip Casson |
| 793 | 29/09/92 | Arnold Yarrow | Philip Casson | 840 | 11/03/93 | Susan Boyd | Philip Casson |
| 794 | 01/10/92 | Lilie Ferrari | Philip Casson | 841 | 16/03/93 | Michael Robartes | Geoff Feld |
| 795 | 06/10/92 | Tony McHale | Barry Letts | 842 | 18/03/93 | Michael Robartes | Geoff Feld |
| 796 | 08/10/92 | Tony McHale | Barry Letts | 843 | 23/03/93 | Tony McHale | Leonard Lewis |
| 797 | 13/10/92 | Ashley Pharoah | Matthew Evans | 844 | 25/03/93 | Tony McHale | Leonard Lewis |
| 798 | 15/10/92 | Ashley Pharoah | Matthew Evans | 845 | 30/03/93 | Tony Jordan | Richard Laxton |
| 799 | 20/10/92 | Tony Jordan | Sue Dunderdale | 846 | 01/04/93 | Tony Jordan | Richard Laxton |
| 800 | 22/10/92 | Tony Jordan | Sue Dunderdale | 847 | 06/04/93 | Arnold Yarrow | Philip Casson |
| 801 | 27/10/92 | Susan Boyd | Garth Tucker | 848 | 08/04/93 | Arnold Yarrow | Philip Casson |
| 802 | 29/10/92 | Susan Boyd | Garth Tucker | 849 | 13/04/93 | Jeff Povey | Bill Hays |
| 803 | 03/11/92 | Gillian Richmond | Mike Dormer | | | | |
| 804 | 05/11/92 | Gillian Richmond | Mike Dormer | | | | |

| Episode | Transmission date | Writer | Director |
|---|---|---|---|
| 850 | 15/04/93 | Jeff Povey | Bill Hays |
| 851 | 20/04/93 | Duncan Gould | Garth Tucker |
| 852 | 22/04/93 | Jonathan Myerson | Garth Tucker |
| 853 | 27/04/93 | Susan Boyd | Gwennan Sage |
| 854 | 29/04/93 | Susan Boyd | Gwennan Sage |
| 855 | 04/05/93 | Kolton Lee | Indra Bhose |
| 856 | 06/05/93 | Kolton Lee | Indra Bhose |
| 857 | 11/05/93 | Tony McHale | Tony McHale |
| 858 | 13/05/93 | Tony McHale | Tony McHale |
| 859 | 18/05/93 | Matthew Graham | Beryl Richards |
| 860 | 20/05/93 | Matthew Graham | Beryl Richards |
| 861 | 25/05/93 | Tony Jordan | Bill Hays |
| 862 | 27/05/93 | Tony Jordan | Bill Hays |
| 863 | 01/06/93 | Jeff Povey | Margy Kinmonth |
| 864 | 03/06/93 | Jeff Povey | Margy Kinmonth |
| 865 | 08/06/93 | Michael Robartes | Bren Simson |
| 866 | 10/06/93 | Michael Robartes | Bren Simson |
| 867 | 15/06/93 | Tony Jordan | Keith Boak |
| 868 | 17/06/93 | Tony Jordan | Keith Boak |
| 869 | 22/06/93 | Lilie Ferrari | Gwennan Sage |
| 870 | 24/06/93 | Lilie Ferrari | Gwennan Sage |
| 871 | 29/06/93 | Susan Boyd | Sue Dunderdale |
| 872 | 01/07/93 | Susan Boyd | Sue Dunderdale |
| 873 | 06/07/93 | Arnold Yarrow | Margy Kinmonth |
| 874 | 08/07/93 | Colin Brake | Margy Kinmonth |
| 875 | 13/07/93 | Joanne Maguire | Bren Simson |
| 876 | 15/07/93 | Barrie Shore | Bren Simson |
| 877 | 20/07/93 | Tony McHale | Ian White |
| 878 | 22/07/93 | Tony McHale | Ian White |
| 879 | 27/07/93 | Tony Jordan | Garth Tucker |
| 880 | 29/07/93 | Tony Jordan | Garth Tucker |
| 881 | 03/08/93 | Michael Robartes | Richard Laxton |
| 882 | 05/08/93 | Michael Robartes | Richard Laxton |
| 883 | 10/08/93 | Jeff Povey | Maggie Ford |
| 884 | 12/08/93 | Jeff Povey | Maggie Ford |
| 885 | 17/08/93 | Deborah Cook | Ian White |
| 886 | 19/08/93 | Deborah Cook | Ian White |
| 887 | 24/08/93 | Susan Boyd | Garth Tucker |
| 888 | 26/08/93 | Susan Boyd | Garth Tucker |
| 889 | 31/08/93 | Tony Jordan | Leonard Lewis |
| 890 | 02/09/93 | Tony Jordan | Leonard Lewis |
| 891 | 07/09/93 | Tony McHale | Keith Boak |
| 892 | 09/09/93 | Tony McHale | Keith Boak |
| 893 | 14/09/93 | Kolton Lee | Bill Hays |
| 894 | 16/09/93 | Colin Brake | Bill Hays |
| 895 | 21/09/93 | Joanne Maguire | Indra Bhose |
| 896 | 23/09/93 | Tony Etchells | Indra Bhose |
| 897 | 28/09/93 | Barrie Shore | Geoff Feld |
| 898 | 30/09/93 | Ashley Pharoah | Geoff Feld |
| 899 | 05/10/93 | Ashley Pharoah | Andrew Morgan |
| 900 | 07/10/93 | Ashley Pharoah | Andrew Morgan |
| 901 | 12/10/93 | Deborah Cook | Bill Hays |
| 902 | 14/10/93 | Deborah Cook | Bill Hays |
| 903 | 19/10/93 | Jeff Povey | Keith Boak |
| 904 | 21/10/93 | Jeff Povey | Keith Boak |
| 905 | 26/10/93 | Susan Boyd | Geoff Feld |
| 906 | 28/10/93 | Susan Boyd | Geoff Feld |
| 907 | 02/11/93 | Michael Robartes | Andrew Morgan |
| 908 | 04/11/93 | Michael Robartes | Andrew Morgan |
| 909 | 09/11/93 | Lisa Evans | Stephen Garwood |
| 910 | 11/11/93 | Tony McHale | Stephen Garwood |
| 911 | 16/11/93 | Tony McHale | Tony McHale |
| 912 | 18/11/93 | Tony McHale | Tony McHale |
| 913 | 23/11/93 | Tony Jordan | Brian Stirner |
| 914 | 25/11/93 | Tony Jordan | Brian Stirner |
| 915 | 30/11/93 | Matthew Graham | Margy Kinmonth |
| 916 | 02/12/93 | Joanne Maguire | Margy Kinmonth |
| 917 | 07/12/93 | Barrie Shore | Jeremy Woolf |
| 918 | 09/12/93 | Barrie Shore | Jeremy Woolf |
| 919 | 14/12/93 | Jeff Povey | Geoff Feld |
| 920 | 16/12/93 | Jeff Povey | Geoff Feld |
| 921 | 21/12/93 | Tony McHale | Ian White |
| 922 | 23/12/93 | Tony McHale | Ian White |
| 922a | 25/12/93 | Tony McHale | Ian White |
| 923 | 28/12/93 | Tony Jordan | Margy Kinmonth |
| 924 | 30/12/93 | Tony Jordan | Margy Kinmonth |
| 925 | 04/01/94 | Tony Jordan | Chris Fallon |
| 926 | 06/01/94 | Tony Etchells | Chris Fallon |
| 927 | 11/01/94 | Deborah Cook | Gwennan Sage |
| 928 | 13/01/94 | Deborah Cook | Gwennan Sage |
| 929 | 18/01/94 | Michael Robartes | Sue Bysh |
| 930 | 20/01/94 | Michael Robartes | Sue Bysh |
| 931 | 25/01/94 | Susan Boyd | Garth Tucker |
| 932 | 27/01/94 | Susan Boyd | Garth Tucker |
| 933 | 01/02/94 | Joanne Maguire | Bill Hays |
| 934 | 03/02/94 | Joanne Maguire | Bill Hays |
| 935 | 08/02/94 | Jeff Povey | Brian Stirner |
| 936 | 10/02/94 | Jeff Povey | Brian Stirner |
| 937 | 15/02/94 | Tony Jordan | Philip Casson |
| 938 | 17/02/94 | Tony Jordan | Philip Casson |
| 939 | 22/02/94 | Tony Jordan | David Innes Edwards |
| 940 | 24/02/94 | Matthew Graham | David Innes Edwards |
| 941 | 01/03/94 | Arnold Yarrow | Bill Hays |
| 942 | 03/03/94 | Colin Brake | Bill Hays |
| 943 | 08/03/94 | Matthew Graham | Jo Johnson |
| 944 | 10/03/94 | Matthew Graham | Jo Johnson |
| 945 | 15/03/94 | Jeff Povey | Philip Casson |
| 946 | 17/03/94 | Jeff Povey | Philip Casson |

| Episode | Transmission date | Writer | Director | Episode | Transmission date | Writer | Director |
|---------|-------------------|--------|----------|---------|-------------------|--------|----------|
| 947 | 22/03/94 | Gillian Richmond | David Innes Edwards | 42 | 14/07/94 | Helen Blizard | Phillip Casson |
| 948 | 24/03/94 | Gillian Richmond | David Innes Edwards | 43 | 18/07/94 | Joanne Maguire | Sue Butterworth |
| | | | | 44 | 19/07/94 | Joanne Maguire | Sue Butterworth |
| 949 | 29/03/94 | Michael Robartes | Adrian Bean | 45 | 21/07/94 | Joanne Maguire | Sue Butterworth |
| 950 | 31/03/94 | Michael Robartes | Adrian Bean | 46 | 25/07/94 | Jeff Povey | Bill Hays |
| 951 | 05/04/94 | Tony McHale | Tony McHale | 47 | 27/07/94 | Jeff Povey | Bill Hays |
| 952 | 07/04/94 | Tony McHale | Tony McHale | 48 | 28/07/94 | Jeff Povey | Bill Hays |
| 1 | 11/04/94 | uncredited | uncredited | 49 | 01/08/94 | Richard Zajdlic | Jeremy Woolf |
| 2 | 12/04/94 | Tony Jordan | Leonard Lewis | 50 | 02/08/94 | Tony Etchells | Jeremy Woolf |
| 3 | 14/04/94 | Ashley Pharoah | Keith Boak | 51 | 04/08/94 | Tony Etchells | Jeremy Woolf |
| 4 | 18/04/94 | Ashley Pharoah | Keith Boak | 52 | 08/08/94 | Matthew Graham | Jo Johnson |
| 5 | 19/04/94 | Ashley Pharoah | Keith Boak | 53 | 09/08/94 | Matthew Graham | Jo Johnson |
| 6 | 21/04/94 | Susan Boyd | Philip Casson | 54 | 11/08/94 | Matthew Graham | Jo Johnson |
| 7 | 25/04/94 | Susan Boyd | Philip Casson | 55 | 15/08/94 | Tony Jordan | Misha Williams |
| 8 | 26/04/94 | Susan Boyd | Philip Casson | 56 | 16/08/94 | Tony Jordan | Misha Williams |
| 9 | 28/04/94 | Jeff Povey | Bill Hays | 57 | 18/08/94 | Tony Jordan | Misha Williams |
| 11 | 03/05/94 | Jeff Povey | Bill Hays | 58 | 22/08/94 | Colin Brake | Penelope Shales |
| 12 | 05/05/94 | Barrie Shore | Bill Hays | 59 | 23/08/94 | Colin Brake | Penelope Shales |
| 13 | 09/05/94 | Joanne Maguire | Geoff Feld | 60 | 25/08/94 | Sian Orwells | Penelope Shales |
| 14 | 10/05/94 | Joanne Maguire | Geoff Feld | 61 | 29/08/94 | Gillian Richmond | Keith Boak |
| 15 | 12/05/94 | Len Collin | Geoff Feld | 62 | 30/08/94 | Gillian Richmond | Keith Boak |
| 16 | 16/05/94 | Tony McHale | Stephen Garwood | 63 | 01/09/94 | Gillian Richmond | Keith Boak |
| 17 | 17/05/94 | Tony McHale | Stephen Garwood | 64 | 05/09/94 | Michael Robartes | Chris Fallon |
| 18 | 19/05/94 | Tony McHale | Stephen Garwood | 65 | 06/09/94 | Michael Robartes | Chris Fallon |
| 19 | 23/05/94 | Gillian Richmond | Penelope Shales | 66 | 08/09/94 | Len Collin | Chris Fallon |
| 20 | 24/05/94 | Gillian Richmond | Penelope Shales | 67 | 12/09/94 | Debbie Cook | Garth Tucker |
| 21 | 26/05/94 | Gillian Richmond | Penelope Shales | 68 | 13/09/94 | Debbie Cook | Garth Tucker |
| 22 | 30/05/94 | Michael Robartes | Jeff Naylor | 69 | 15/09/94 | Debbie Cook | Garth Tucker |
| 23 | 31/05/94 | Arnold Yarrow | Jeff Naylor | 70 | 19/09/94 | Barrie Shore | Brian Stirner |
| 24 | 02/06/94 | Tony Etchells | Jeff Naylor | 71 | 20/09/94 | Barrie Shore | Brian Stirner |
| 25 | 06/06/94 | Susan Boyd | Chris Fallon | 72 | 22/09/94 | Barrie Shore | Brian Stirner |
| 26 | 07/06/94 | Susan Boyd | Chris Fallon | 73 | 26/09/94 | Joanne Maguire | Sue Bysh |
| 27 | 09/06/94 | Susan Boyd | Chris Fallon | 74 | 27/09/94 | Joanne Maguire | Sue Bysh |
| 28 | 13/06/94 | Tony Jordan | Keith Boak | 75 | 29/09/94 | Joanne Maguire | Sue Bysh |
| 29 | 14/06/94 | Tony Jordan | Keith Boak | 76 | 03/10/94 | Helen Blizzard | Jo Johnson |
| 30 | 16/06/94 | Tony Jordan | Keith Boak | 77 | 04/10/94 | Tony Jordan | Jo Johnson |
| 31 | 20/06/94 | Barrie Shore | John Darnell | 78 | 06/10/94 | Tony Etchells | Jo Johnson |
| 32 | 21/06/94 | Barrie Shore | John Darnell | 79 | 10/10/94 | Jeff Povey | Chris Miller |
| 33 | 23/06/94 | Colin Brake | John Darnell | 80 | 11/10/94 | Jeff Povey | Chris Miller |
| 34 | 27/06/94 | Ashley Pharoah | Gwennan Sage | 81 | 13/10/94 | Jeff Povey | Chris Miller |
| 35 | 28/06/94 | Ashley Pharoah | Gwennan Sage | 82 | 17/10/94 | Sue Boyd | Geoff Feld |
| 36 | 30/06/94 | Ashley Pharoah | Gwennan Sage | 83 | 18/10/94 | Sue Boyd | Geoff Feld |
| 37 | 04/07/94 | Susan Boyd | Bill Gilmour | 84 | 20/10/94 | Sue Boyd | Geoff Feld |
| 38 | 05/07/94 | Susan Boyd | Bill Gilmour | 85 | 24/10/94 | Tony Jordan | Chris Fallon |
| 39 | 07/07/94 | Susan Boyd | Bill Gilmour | 86 | 25/10/94 | Tony Jordan | Chris Fallon |
| 40 | 11/07/94 | Debbie Cook | Phillip Casson | 87 | 27/10/94 | Tony Jordan | Chris Fallon |
| 41 | 12/07/94 | Debbie Cook | Phillip Casson | 88 | 31/10/94 | Tony Etchells | Gwenan Sage |

# Index